Nobody Loves Me

Also by Maggie Hartley

Nobody Loves Me

BOBBY'S TRUE STORY OF NEGLECT, SECRETS AND ABUSE

MAGGIE HARTLEY

WITH
HEATHER BISHOP

SEVEN DIALS

First published in Great Britain in 2023 by Seven Dials,
an imprint of The Orion Publishing Group Ltd
Carmelite House, 50 Victoria Embankment
London EC4Y 0DZ

An Hachette UK Company

1 3 5 7 9 10 8 6 4 2

A CIP catalogue record for this book is
available from the British Library.

ISBN (Mass Market Paperback) 978 1 3996 0660 8
ISBN (Audiobook) 978 1 3996 0662 2
ISBN (eBook) 978 1 3996 0661 5

Typeset by Born Group
Printed and bound in Great Britain by Clays Ltd, Elcograf S.p.A.

www.orionbooks.co.uk

Dedication

This book is dedicated to Bobby, Poppy and Melodie and all the children who have passed through my home. It's been a privilege to have cared for you and to be able to share your stories.

Contents

A Message from Maggie

I wanted to write this book to give people an honest account about what it's like to be a foster carer; to talk about some of the challenges that I face on a day-to-day basis and some of the children that I've helped.

My main concern throughout all this is to protect the children who have been in my care. For this reason, all names and identifying details have been changed, including my own, and no locations have been included. All my stories are based on real-life experiences I have been through.

Being a foster carer is a privilege and I couldn't imagine doing anything else. My house is never quiet but I wouldn't have it any other way. I hope perhaps my stories inspire other people to consider fostering, as new carers are always desperately needed. In fact, the latest statistics are alarming. Ofsted figures from 2022 showed that the number of available homes for foster children in England had fallen by almost a quarter in four years. This comes at the same time as the number of children in the UK care system is at a record high. Foster carers are needed more than ever, so please do look into it if it's something that you or someone you know has ever considered. Fostering is one way in which we can all help make sure no one is left behind.

Maggie Hartley

ONE

New Beginnings

The only way to describe my house today was utter chaos. As someone who always likes to be organised, it made me feel very twitchy.

'Come on, boys,' I said enthusiastically. 'Your social worker will be here soon and she's going to take you back home.'

'You want to be all ready to see Mummy, don't you?'

Three little heads with the most gorgeous hair nodded back at me and I smiled. I couldn't be cross with them if I tried.

For the past three weeks I'd been looking after three brothers: six-year-old AJ, and four-year-old twins, Samuel and Tristan. It was respite care while their mum, Di, had been to Trinidad to see her mother who was terminally ill.

Di was a single parent who had escaped from a relationship with the boys' father, a drug addict. She had also struggled with her own mental health problems, so Social Services had been giving her ongoing support since the boys were small. She didn't want to take them out of school and she couldn't afford four plane tickets, but she didn't have any other family in the UK who could look after them, so that's where I came in. As a foster carer for over twenty years, I often did respite care between long-term placements. I look after children from anything from a few days to a few months while their parents or carers are in hospital, or if they needed a break if their child had physical or mental disabilities. Or, like Di, a family situation came up where they needed my help.

They were lovely boys, but so full of energy and always on the go. Coupled with that, the twins were not great sleepers and especially being away from home, they'd missed their mum, so I'd had several wake-ups every night. There was also the school run to do every morning and getting the three of them out of the door and into the car for the thirty-minute journey to their primary school had been a challenge. To be honest, I was exhausted!

'They are gorgeous children but I'm ready for a lie-down,' I'd joked to Becky, my supervising social worker at the fostering agency that I worked for, when she'd called last night. Now they were heading home to see their mum, I knew I was going to miss them.

They were leaving with one more bag than they'd arrived with. I knew that Di struggled financially and the boys' clothes were very worn and tired and I could tell they'd already had previous owners. So I'd taken them to my local ASDA and kitted them out. I didn't want to go overboard and make Di feel uncomfortable, so I'd just bought a few basics for each of them – a winter coat, some pyjamas, a couple of jumpers and jogging bottoms and some new underwear and socks.

I'd taken all the tags off and when I packed all of their stuff into a bag, I'd added a little note to explain.

Hi Di, I hope you don't mind but I had a few spare clothes
in my cupboards that I needed to get rid of so I gave a few
bits to the boys. Maggie x

I'd met Di before she'd left for Trinidad and, despite her
struggles, I could tell she was a great mum. The boys were
bright, polite and well cared for.

However, they were also very messy. The kitchen floor was
covered in a sea of toy cars, board games and Transformers.
While I'd been packing, they had been playing – seemingly
with every toy I had in my cupboard.

After we'd all thrown a few things into my plastic toy boxes,
it was clear that that was as good as it was going to get.

'I'm going to miss you three,' I told them as I wrestled
them into their coats. 'My house is going to seem very quiet
without you. But I know you're not going to miss me because
you're going to see Mummy.'

Tristan's brown eyes lit up.

'Yay! We're going to see Mummy,' he smiled.

'You certainly are,' I said. 'And I bet she has missed you
so much.'

'I've missed her too,' said AJ.

As well as being the eldest, he was the quieter, more
sensitive of the three boys.

As Di didn't have a car, they were being picked up by their
social worker, Jane, and taken back to their flat.

'Now, Jane's going to be here any minute to take you to
Mummy,' I told them. 'Do any of you need the toilet?'

They shook their heads.

'Are you sure?' I asked as I could see Tristan doing what

3

I'd come to recognise as the little dance he did when he desperately needed a wee.

'Come on, Tristy,' I said. 'Let's go and try, just in case.'

I was just helping him dry his hands when there was a knock at the door.

'That will be Jane,' I yelled.

Sure enough, Jane, a friendly, kind woman in her forties, was standing there.

'Hello there,' she grinned. 'Are you ready to go, boys? Mummy's waiting for you at home.'

I gave them each a cuddle.

'It's been lovely getting to know you boys,' I said to them. 'Enjoy being back home with Mummy.'

'Can we come back and play with your cars again?' asked Samuel.

'Of course you can, flower,' I smiled. 'Your mum can pop round for a cup of tea and you can come for a play whenever you want.'

They all nodded. I could see they were now desperate to get in the car and get home.

I got the boys into car seats in the back of Jane's car while she loaded their stuff into the back.

'They're going home with one extra bag,' I explained to her. 'There's a couple of books and their favourite cars that they got attached to that I want them to have. Plus a few bits of clothes that I had lying around.'

'That's kind of you, Maggie,' she smiled. 'I'm sure Di will appreciate that.'

'I'm sure it's always a struggle with three mouths to feed,' I replied.

As she drove off, three little faces peered at me through the window.

'Bye boys!' I waved.

They'd only been with me a few short weeks but I knew I was going to miss them terribly. However, as I walked back into the quiet house, I sank down onto the sofa and gave myself a few minutes to enjoy the peace.

It had been an easy placement in terms of the fact that the boys hadn't suffered abuse, neglect or trauma. Naturally they had missed their mum and at first they were unsure about being in a new place with someone who was effectively a stranger to them, but, unlike many of the children that I fostered, they were happy, settled children and they'd adapted well.

As I cleared away the rest of the cars and Transformers, I couldn't help but wonder who the next child or children to come through my door would be.

Now the boys had gone, Becky would be putting me back on the available list for fosterers, so I imagined it wouldn't be too long before I got a call. Sadly, the need is so great for foster carers, particularly experienced ones like me who had been doing it for years, that it's rarely more than a few days before I'm offered a new placement.

I didn't know whether to box up the toys and put them back in the loft or leave them for the time being. Over the years I'd been fostering, I'd collected toys and games to suit all ages, from babies right up to teens. I'd adapt my collection depending on the age of the children that I was fostering at the time. I decided to leave them for now until I knew more about who my next placement would be.

I stripped all of the beds and put the towels in the wash. All three of the boys had shared the largest bedroom that I used for fostering, where there was a bunk bed as well as a single bed. I found cleaning therapeutic and it was always part of my ritual when a child or children left. I gave the room a good clean, dust and a hoover.

I'd just stopped for lunch when my mobile rang. It was Louisa.

Louisa had come to me as a thirteen-year-old after her parents had tragically died in a car crash. She'd stayed with me for years and I treated her as if she was my own biological daughter. She was now married to Charlie and they had an adorable eighteen-month-old called Edie. Louisa was a nanny to a local family and she and Edie would often pop in on their walk home from work.

'Hi Maggie, have the boys gone?' she asked.

'Yes, they went off fine first thing this morning,' I told her.

'Edie's been asking for you,' she told me. 'Would you mind if we popped in on the way home tonight?'

'Course not,' I said. 'You're welcome any time, you know that. You can stay for a bit of dinner if you want.'

'If you're sure?'

'Of course I'm sure,' I told her. 'I've been used to cooking for four for the past few weeks so I'll rustle something up for us.'

'Great – see you later,' she said.

I looked forward to seeing her and I would never turn down a chance for Nana cuddles with Edie. When a placement left, the house always felt eerily quiet for a day or two, so it would be nice to have some company.

I spent the rest of the afternoon cleaning, tidying and making a pasta bake, as I knew that was one of Edie's favourites.

It was just before five-thirty when my mobile rang.

That will be Louisa telling me she's on her way, I thought to myself, as I went to answer it.

But it wasn't Louisa's voice on the other end.

'Oh,' I said. 'Hi Becky.'

'Sorry, Maggie,' she said. 'I know you weren't expecting me.'

'No no, that's fine,' I said. 'I thought it was Louisa, that's all. She's due to come round and I didn't look at the number.'

I assumed she was ringing to check on the boys.

'What can I do for you? The boys all went off fine this morning,' I told her. 'I felt quite sad saying good bye to them but they were so excited about seeing their mum, bless them.'

'Oh, I'm glad,' she said.

She paused.

'I'm not actually ringing about the boys, Maggie,' she told me. 'I wanted to talk to you about another placement.'

'That's fine,' I told her. 'When are you looking for it to start?'

'Well, now,' she said. 'It's a sibling group that need an emergency placement.'

If children were thought to be at risk of being harmed, they were immediately taken into the care system.

I listened, taking it all in as Becky began to explain more.

'It's three children again, Maggie,' she told me.

'That's OK,' I said. 'I've had plenty of practice.'

She explained that all she knew was that it was two girls and a boy and something had happened at their primary school today that had led to suspicions of neglect.

'The head teacher called Social Services and they kept all three kids at school until social workers could speak to their parents, and I think they got quite a hostile reception.'

Becky didn't have any more details about the children or the allegations.

'Obviously, as you know, it's very early days and this might amount to nothing,' she told me. 'They might just be with you for a night or two while this gets sorted out. Or it could be longer than that.'

With emergency placements like this, it was always going to be the unknown.

'What do you think, Maggie?' she asked me. 'Would you consider taking them?'

I didn't need to think about it. I had the space and I could never turn away children who were possibly at risk of harm and were in desperate need of a safe place to go.

'Of course,' I said. 'I'll need to get the beds made up again but we'll muddle through for tonight. Do you know when they're likely to be here?'

'Imminently,' she said. 'Once Social Services know there's a carer willing to take them, their social worker will bring them round to you.'

'Do you know their names?' I asked her.

'I'm afraid I don't,' replied Becky. 'All I know is their social worker is called Patsy. I'll tell her to give you a call.'

The name was familiar.

'Is she an Irish lady?' I asked. 'I think I've worked with her before, years ago.'

'Yes, come to think of it, she did have an Irish accent on the phone,' said Becky.

I'd just put the phone down when there was a knock at the door.

Louisa.

I'd forgotten she was coming. As I opened it, Edie grinned up at me from her pushchair.

'Na Na Na,' she beamed, holding out her arms to me.

'Yes, it's Nana,' I smiled. 'Hello lovey.'

I unclipped the straps and she leapt into my arms. But after a quick cuddle, she pulled away and toddled off towards the kitchen.

'She knows where the toys are,' laughed Louisa.

'I'm afraid this might have to be a bit of a quick visit,' I explained to her. 'Becky's just called me.'

I explained what had happened.

'Oh don't worry, we can go and leave you to it,' Louisa told me. 'You must have loads to sort out.'

'To be honest, the social worker hasn't even rung me yet,' I said. 'There's a pasta bake keeping warm in the oven so it's no trouble.'

'As long as you're sure,' she said. 'I don't want the kids to suddenly arrive with us sitting here.'

'There's time for a quick dinner,' I replied.

I was suddenly pleased that I'd made a big portion as it meant there would be enough left over in case the children arriving on my doorstep were hungry.

I had one eye on my phone as I lifted Edie into a highchair and put a plastic bowl of pasta down in front of her.

'Nana's made you your favourite,' I told her.

'Thanks so much for doing this,' said Louisa. 'I'm always shattered when I get in from work and by the time I've fed

Edie and put her to bed, I don't have any energy left to make me and Charlie tea.'

'It's my pleasure, lovey,' I said.

Louisa noticed me checking my phone which I'd put down next to me on the dining table.

'Any news?' she asked.

'No,' I shrugged. 'Nothing yet.'

It was a cold winter's night and my heart went out to those three poor children. They would have been at school nearly four hours extra now, probably hungry, tired and scared, and wondering why they weren't allowed to go home. Even in the most horrific situations of neglect, home was still their familiar.

As I tidied away the dinner plates, there was still no news from Patsy.

'Edie and I will get off now and leave you to it,' Louisa told me.

'I'm sorry it's been a bit rushed, lovey,' I smiled.

'Don't be silly, I know you must have loads to sort out,' she replied. 'I hope that it goes OK.'

As soon as I'd strapped Edie back in her pushchair and waved them off, I got to work. I was glad that I'd spent the day cleaning and sorting but there was still a lot more left to do.

I wanted to make the house as warm and welcoming as possible for them. As well as the big bedroom that the boys had been in, I had another smaller single room that I used for fostering.

I thought I'd put the girls in the big room and the boy in the single room, although I knew they might want to stay together, especially on their first night. Siblings often cling to each other for comfort when they first get taken into care.

I made all the beds with fresh bedding and put hot water bottles in each one just to make them nice and cosy. I placed a fleecy blanket on the end of each bed along with a little teddy bear.

I wasn't sure of their exact ages but Becky had told me they were all coming from a primary school so I knew they would all be eleven or under.

I went into my big cupboard and rummaged around for some pyjamas in sizes that might work for them. Even if I didn't have clothes for their exact ages, I had enough stuff that we could make do for one night. Pyjama bottoms and sleeves could always be rolled up. I always had a big stash of toothbrushes and toiletries that I picked up when they were on offer at the supermarket.

I'd just finished getting some towels out when my replace rang. I quickly pounced on it.

'Maggie Hartley?' said a woman with a thick Irish accent. 'It's Patsy here from Social Services.'

'Hi Patsy, I said. 'How's it going?'

'I'm finally on my way with the children,' she said. 'I'm sorry it's taken so long.'

'How are they?' I asked.

'As you'd expect,' she said in a hushed voice. 'Tired, bewildered and confused. I can't say much now, Maggie, because they're here in the car with me, but we can have a quick chat when we arrive.'

'No problem,' I said. 'See you soon.'

I realised after I hung up that I still hadn't asked their names. I'd have to wait now until they arrived.

Even though I'd done this so many times over the years, I always had a churning feeling in the pit of my stomach when I was waiting for a new child to arrive. It was a strange mixture of nerves and anticipation about what kind of situation I was going to face.

All I could think about was those three bewildered children sat in the back of the social worker's car wondering what was going to happen to them. I couldn't even imagine what that must feel like and how scary it would be for a little one.

Suddenly there was a loud knock on the front door that made me jump.

This was it. They were here and I was as ready as I could be. I went to answer it, filled with apprehension about what I was about to be faced with.

TWO

Into the Unknown

Stood on the doorstep was a woman in her thirties with dark curly hair wearing bright red lipstick. She was fashionably dressed with wide jeans, a striped jumper and a smart navy blue coat.

'Patsy?' I asked.

She looked so familiar but I couldn't place her.

'We've met before, haven't we?' I said and she nodded.

'Oh yes,' she said. 'I thought I recognised your name. You looked after Missy while we tried to find her a new placement.'

'Aah that's right,' I smiled. 'Sorry, my memory is terrible sometimes.'

'Oh don't worry, it was quite a few years ago now,' Patsy replied.

Missy had been a ten-year-old girl with autism and a lot of behavioural issues. She'd accused her foster carers of hitting her and, while the allegations were being investigated, she'd been immediately removed. She'd come to live with me in what was known as a bridging placement. In the end, things had broken down so badly with her former foster parents that she was moved to another carer. But it had taken nearly two months to find someone suitable who would take her on.

I couldn't keep her long-term as I already had Louisa with me permanently and I knew Missy needed one-to-one attention.

Back then, Patsy was a newly qualified social worker but she was good at her job and we'd got along well.

'How's Missy doing?' I asked her. 'Are you still her social worker?'

'Yes, I am,' smiled Patsy. 'She still has her challenges but she's moved to a specialist residential school now where she really seems to have settled.'

'I'm glad to hear it,' I nodded.

Although I would have loved to chat more, my mind suddenly focused back on the situation we were dealing with now. The one thing I'd noticed was that Patsy was standing on the doorstep alone.

'Where are the children?' I asked her, puzzled.

'Oh they're in the car,' she told me, gesturing to a red Nissan parked outside my house.

'I wanted to keep them out of the cold and have a quick word with you before I brought them in.'

'How are they doing?' I asked her.

'Tired, fed up and, as you'd imagine, very bewildered,' she shrugged.

I knew we couldn't leave them in the car for long so Patsy quickly ran through the basics. As Becky had said, it was a sibling group of three: Melodie was eleven, Poppy, ten, and there was eight-year-old Bobby.

'The school rang us this morning about suspicions of neglect,' she explained. 'The parents are hostile and clearly aren't willing to cooperate with us at this point so we had no choice but to go for an EPO.'

If Social Services believe that a child is in immediate danger, they can apply to the courts for an Emergency Protection Order, known as an EPO. A judge is always on call to deal with these and they can rush them through in a matter of hours.

I had so many questions but before Patsy could tell me any more, we heard someone knocking. In the glow of the street light, I could just make out a girl's face peering out of the back window of the car. She was tapping impatiently on the glass.

'I'd better go and bring them in as they'll be getting cold,' Patsy said, quickly heading off down the path.

I couldn't make out much in the gloom outside but I saw Patsy getting two purple rucksacks and a carrier bag out of the boot. Then a boy headed towards me up the path. He was small and looked much younger than eight.

'Hi, you must be Bobby,' I said gently. 'I'm Maggie.'

As I spoke, he looked up at me.

His blue eyes were big, blank and expressionless, and there were dark shadows underneath them. He had a thin face and his skin was so pale, it was almost translucent.

'Come on in and get warm,' I told him.

He wasn't wearing a coat and I could see that he was shivering.

His school uniform was an odd mishmash. His dirty trousers hung off him and were so long, they were trailing on the floor and had big holes in both knees. His blue school jumper was so small the sleeves finished at his elbows and it only went as far as his upper waist so it looked like a crop top. His shoes were tatty and worn and had split at the toes.

'Maggie, this is Bobby,' said Patsy, bustling up the path behind him.

'We've already met,' I smiled.

He stood in the hallway, not saying a word, staring down at the floor.

'And this is Melodie and Poppy,' said Patsy as she ushered the two girls forwards into the light of the hallway.

I was so surprised, I almost did a double take. I'd expected them to be pale, scruffy and thin just like their brother. But they were tall and heavyset with full faces and pink cheeks. Their eyes were bright and their long brown hair looked clean and glossy. They were both wearing matching pink puffer jackets and shiny black patent shoes.

'I'm Maggie,' I smiled. 'Come on in.'

'Do we have to?' scowled the taller girl who I assumed was the oldest, Melodie.

'I've explained this to you, Melodie,' Patsy told her patiently. 'Let's get you inside out of the cold and I'll go through it with you again.'

Her sister, Poppy, looked equally unimpressed.

'Let me take your coats,' I told the girls and they handed me their pink puffas.

'Did you bring a coat, Bobby?' I asked him but he looked down at the floor.

'I don't think Bobby had one with him or if he did, we've accidentally left it at school,' said Patsy.

'Not to worry,' I smiled. 'I've got plenty of warm coats in my cupboards.'

I led them into the living room at the front of the house. The girls flopped down on the sofa but Bobby stood there, his eyes still lowered to the floor.

'You can sit down too, flower,' I told him gently, leading him over to a chair.

There was a frailty about him – almost like if you touched him, he might break.

'I know you must all be hungry but I need to have a quick chat with Patsy,' I told them. 'So I'll get you a juice and a biscuit now and then I'll get you some dinner later.'

'I don't want nothing to eat,' scowled Poppy. 'I want to go home to Mummy.'

'I'm afraid that's not possible at the moment,' Patsy explained. 'Remember that we said you're going to stay the night at Maggie's house. We'll know more tomorrow when we talk to your parents.'

'I hate talking,' sighed Melodie. 'I just want to go back to our flat.'

'I can completely understand that,' I smiled sympathetically. 'And Patsy will let us know what's going on as soon as she can, but tonight you're going to stay here with me.'

The girls sat back begrudgingly. Patsy put the TV on and got them settled while I quickly got them a glass of juice and a biscuit from the kitchen.

When I came back in, *You've Been Framed* was on and they all seem transfixed.

'Maggie and I are just going to have a quick chat in the kitchen,' Patsy told them.

'We're only next door so shout out to us if you need anything,' I added.

None of them said a word as their eyes stayed glued to the screen.

Back in the kitchen, I put the kettle on and made Patsy and myself a cup of tea.

'Have the children eaten anything?' I asked her.

'Not really, just some snacky stuff at school,' she said.

'I've got a pasta bake keeping warm in the oven so I'll give that to them when you've gone,' I told her.

When the tea had brewed, I took it over to Patsy and sat down at the table with her.

'Thanks so much,' she sighed. 'It's been a long old afternoon.'

'So tell me what you know,' I said.

Patsy explained that teachers at the school had been concerned about Bobby for a while.

'Apparently he's extremely quiet and withdrawn and often wets himself. As you probably noticed yourself, Maggie, he's incredibly thin and his clothes are very tatty and dirty.'

She explained that teachers had called home a number of times to try to speak to his parents but no one ever got back to them and they had never turned up for his parents' evenings.

'What about the two girls?' I asked. 'Have their teachers noticed anything?'

'Well, that's the weird thing,' said Patsy. 'They don't have any obvious concerns about the girls, either about their appearance or behaviour. They're always clean and well turned out. They're engaged in class and I think Mum has been to school to see their teachers.'

She took a gulp of tea.

'But as you and I know, Maggie, girls are often better at hiding things so who knows what's really going on at home behind closed doors.'

She explained that the family wasn't previously known to Social Services and they'd had no involvement with the children before today.

'So why did the school call you?' I asked.

Patsy explained that when Bobby had been doing PE this morning, his class teacher had noticed bruises at the tops of both of his arms.

'They looked like fingertip bruises,' she told me. 'Like he'd been grabbed. There were also a couple of older, more faded bruises on his back.'

'Did they ask him how he'd got them?'

'Yes, but he didn't say very much or offer any reasonable explanation,' she replied. 'I think that combined with all of the concerns they'd been having about him anyway led his teacher to speak to the safeguarding person at school and she called Social Services.'

Patsy had gone up to the school and spoken to the teachers and then to Bobby.

'I asked him about the bruises and how he'd got them but, as I say, he didn't really say anything,' she told me. 'Then I spoke to the girls to ask them if they knew what had happened. They just told me that Bobby was silly and got into trouble all the time.'

The school had obtained one contact number for Mum, and Patsy had tried that but couldn't get through. So her manager had sent another social worker round to the flat.

'Mum answered, but she refused to engage or let the social worker in. There was lots of swearing, lots of claims that Bobby was a liar and that no one had done anything to him.

'There is a dad around apparently but there was no sign of him.'

The social worker had made it clear to the mother that none of the children would be returning home until they'd found out more.

'She explained that it was significant bruising, along with the concerns from school, which meant they needed to look into it more.'

'What did Mum say?' I asked.

'Nothing,' Patsy replied. 'She just slammed the door in my colleague's face.'

They'd spoken to their manager but they felt there was no other option at this stage than to go for an EPO.

'We've also got to involve the police now, so they'll probably go round tomorrow and see if that forces Mum to engage with us.'

Social Services' main priority is always to keep children safe, so even if there is the smallest element of doubt, they always prefer to err on the side of caution.

'Have they been examined by a medical professional?' I asked Patsy.

'Bobby has,' she replied. 'There's no indication the girls have been harmed so we didn't want to put them through an examination at this stage.'

Patsy had taken Bobby to see a GP. Social Services have a number of GPs in each area who work for them and are based at different medical centres.

The doctor examined Bobby and took photographs of his bruising.

He was underweight and small for his age, but thankfully there were no other obvious injuries except for the bruises. The GP had agreed the bruises looked like grab marks and were more than likely made by adult-sized fingers rather than something that would have happened if Bobby was playing with other children.

'The main aim this afternoon was to get them to a safe place for the night then we'll start looking into things again in the morning,' Patsy told me.

'No problem,' I said. 'And what are your thoughts about school tomorrow?'

'I think it's best they don't go in as we'll need to speak to the parents again and the police might want to talk to the children.'

That was a relief for me to hear. I knew the three of them would probably be exhausted after everything that had happened today and the idea of getting them all up and out the door to a school I'd never been to before would have felt like a real mission.

'Obviously they haven't come with any belongings or clothes except their school stuff,' Patsy told me.

'That's OK,' I smiled. 'I've got enough stuff in my cupboards so that we can make do tonight.'

It was getting late and I wanted to try to get the children fed and as settled as possible for the night. When we went back into the living room, they were still glued to the TV.

'I'm going to go now,' Patsy told them. 'But Maggie's going to look after you and I will see you tomorrow.'

They all looked shell-shocked and none of them said anything as I went to the front door to see Patsy out.

'I hope they're OK tonight,' she told me. 'I know the girls in particular are not happy but it's a situation that needs to be explored.'

'I'm sure they'll be fine,' I told her. 'Let's see what tomorrow brings.'

In these kinds of cases, no one knew what was going to happen. Sometimes when parents had calmed down, they were able to give an adequate explanation and the children were allowed to go home. A lot of the time in fostering, you were dealing with the unknown.

As I waved Patsy off, I felt slightly apprehensive about what the night ahead was going to bring. I had three worried, tired, and traumatised children sitting in my house and I was a complete stranger to them. All I could do was try my hardest to reassure them and make them feel as comfortable and settled as possible.

That was often the nature of being a foster carer. You had to be patient as you rarely got answers straight away.

I had to focus on the here and now. And that was getting them fed, washed and into bed. Then we would have to wait and see what tomorrow would bring.

THREE

Settling In

My mind was whirring with all of the things I needed to do.

'First things first, Maggie,' I told myself.

I knew the children would be starving so I needed to get them fed.

I went to the living room to tell them that I was going to sort them out some dinner, but as I was about to push open the door, I could hear the girls talking.

'I don't like it here,' I heard Poppy mutter. 'I wanna go home. When can we go home, Melodie?'

'I don't know,' she replied. 'It's all that liar cry baby's fault.'

'Yeah, he's a stupid liar,' complained Poppy.

'No, I'm not,' I heard Bobby say.

When I walked back in the room, everyone went quiet.

Bobby looked down at the floor and Melodie scowled at me. I had to say something about what I'd just heard as it wasn't fair for them to put the blame on Bobby.

'Girls, none of this is Bobby's fault,' I told them gently.

'I know you must all feel very scared right now but Social Services have decided that you need to come here. They feel that this needs to happen to keep you safe. Patsy's going to come and see you tomorrow and you can ask her any questions that you want to then, OK?'

The girls nodded.

'Now you must all be hungry so let's go to the kitchen and I'll get you some dinner.'

Yes, the girls were being cruel to Bobby but I knew this was traumatic for all of them. They were looking for someone to blame for the situation they had suddenly found themselves in.

Children all react very differently when they enter the care system. Some are quiet and scared, others are very loud and vocal. Every child was different and they handled the stress in different ways.

I'd heard them bickering but I couldn't imagine being in their shoes and suddenly arriving in the cold and dark on a stranger's doorstep. I usually found with children who were very mouthy that it was often a front to cover up their nerves.

I got them sat down around the table and dished them out a plate of pasta bake each.

'Tuck in,' I told them, as I got them a drink of water each.

Melodie pushed the food around her plate.

'Don't like this,' she said.

'What's them bits in it?' asked Poppy.

'That's just onions and pepper,' I told her.

She put down her fork and pushed her plate away.

Meanwhile, Bobby couldn't get the food into his mouth quickly enough. Within minutes, he'd cleared his entire plate.

'Would you like some more, sweetie?' I asked him when he'd finished.

'No, he's not allowed more,' said Melodie firmly. 'He's greedy.'

I assumed that she was worried there would be none left for them. Children who came into the care system were often anxious about food if it had been scarce at home, even if they didn't particularly like it.

'Don't worry, there's enough left for everyone so Bobby can have seconds if he wants,' I reassured her.

'I don't want no more,' said Melodie. 'It's yucky.'

'Would you like some more, Bobby?' I asked and he nodded.

I dished up another portion and he tucked into it.

I wasn't offended that the girls didn't like the food; I could see that they were exhausted and probably just needed to sleep.

Poppy slumped on the table with her head in her hands.

'I want to go home,' she said sadly. 'When can we go back? Can that other lady come and get us and take us home?'

I could hear the desperation in her voice and I really felt for her.

'I know it's really hard for you to understand but you're going to stay here tonight and then let's see what happens in the morning,' I told them. 'You'll hopefully be able to see Mummy and Daddy soon.'

As I said that, I saw Melodie and Poppy scowl.

'Are you missing Mummy too?' I asked Bobby, trying to involve him in the conversation.

'She's not his mummy,' sighed Melodie impatiently. 'She's *our* mum. He hasn't got a mum.'

'Yeah, and Lee's not our dad,' added Poppy. 'We've got another daddy who lives a long way away.'

'Oh I see,' I said, trying to take it all in. 'One of you is going to have to write all of this down for me tomorrow because I'll never remember who's who.'

'But you said we wouldn't be here tomorrow,' yelled Melodie.

'No, flower, I said we would know more tomorrow when Patsy has had time to talk to your parents,' I told her gently.

It was a difficult situation for them to understand and they were bound to be distressed.

By the time I'd cleared away the dishes it was after nine o'clock and I knew I needed to get the children to bed as it would probably take them some time to settle. As I always did, I started with the youngest first.

'Come on, Bobby,' I smiled. 'Come upstairs with me and I'll show you your bedroom.

'Girls, are you OK watching TV while Bobby has a bath?'

'How come he gets his own bedroom?' said Melodie. 'That's not fair!'

'I've got two children's bedrooms in my house,' I told her. 'So it makes sense to have you and Poppy in one room and Bobby in the other.'

Because of safeguarding rules, I generally always put boys and girls in separate rooms. The only exception to that was for the under-fives, who, as long as they didn't disturb each other, I could put in together for comfort and security. Sometimes, if kids shared a room at home and were really insistent, I would let them share in my house if they were under ten. But generally, the local authority and my agency felt that boys and girls were better off separated to avoid any potential issues.

'Come on then, Bobby,' I said. 'Let's go and find you a new toothbrush and some pyjamas.'

He reluctantly stood up and followed me, still not saying anything and avoiding eye contact.

I went through my cupboards and checked what I'd got.

'You're in luck,' I smiled, passing him some age-seven pyjamas that I knew would easily fit him.

I held out my basket of toothbrushes but I could see he was struggling to pick one.

'Here's a nice red one,' I smiled, doing it for him.

The girls had done all of the talking and he'd hardly said a word so far. Now the girls were downstairs and I'd got him on his own, I was keen to check that he was doing OK.

'I'm really glad that you enjoyed your tea,' I told him. 'You'll have to let me know what sort of food you like so I know what to cook. What are your favourites?'

He looked up at me with his vacant blue eyes.

'Sausages,' he whispered.

'Oh, you like sausages?' I asked and he nodded. 'Well, that's good because I happen to have a packet of sausages in my fridge, so how about when we get up in the morning we have sausage sandwiches for breakfast?'

Bobby nodded and I was sure I saw a tiny hint of a smile in the corners of his mouth.

'I'm going to run you a bath now,' I told him. 'Then it will be time for bed. Would you like me to put some bubbles in it?' I asked. 'You know what, I might even have some blue bubble bath in my cupboard. Have you ever had a blue bubble bath before?'

He shook his head.

'Blue bubbles,' he repeated.

He was eight but he seemed much younger.

'You get yourself undressed and I'll find some towels for you when you get out of the bath,' I told him. 'If you need me to help you, just yell.'

I got some towels out of the cupboard on the landing. When I went back in, Bobby was already sitting in the bath, staring in wonder at the blue bubbles.

'Do you like the bubbles?' I asked him and he nodded.

The first thing I noticed were the bright blue bruises at the tops of each of his arms. They stood out against the paleness of his skin. They definitely looked like fingertip marks – as if someone had grabbed him too hard. I knew the GP had already taken photographs of them for Social Services. I could also see some faded yellowy marks on his back. They certainly didn't look like the type of bruises that could have been caused by him accidentally banging into something. I couldn't help but wonder who had done this to him? What had he been through that he wasn't telling anyone about?

'You give yourself a good wash,' I told him, handing him a flannel.

As Bobby stuck one leg out of the water to wash his feet, I caught a glimpse of his toenails and shuddered. They were long and yellowy with a thick crust of dirt in them.

'I'm just going to get my nail clippers and I'll sort your toenails out,' I told him.

He sat there patiently while I clipped them. His fingernails were the same and they clearly hadn't been cut for a long time either.

'I'll leave the clippers out so I can do your sisters' later,' I told him.

'I'm going to wash your hair now. I'll put some shampoo on and rinse it off.'

As I tilted his head back to wet his hair, I could tell it was a while since it had been washed. It was so dry and brittle.

Ten minutes later, Bobby was all clean and the bath water was now a grimy shade of brown.

'Right flower, I've put a towel on the side,' I told him. 'You get yourself out of the bath and get yourself dry and I will go and get your pyjamas.'

When I came back in, Bobby was all wrapped up in his blue towel. He looked so little and vulnerable. His face was etched with tiredness and he had bags under his eyes.

'Let's go and get you settled in your bedroom,' I told him.

I'd put the lamp on in the corner so it looked cosy and there was a neutral navy and white striped duvet on the bed. The sheets were still nice and warm from the hot water bottle.

After he got dressed, he got into bed and looked around anxiously.

'Do you want me to leave the door open a little bit?' I asked him and he nodded.

He looked totally and utterly bewildered.

'You can read some books if you like, just for a little bit while I settle the girls.'

He nodded.

I handed him a couple of the picture books that I'd put on his bedside table.

'Goodnight sweetie,' I told him. 'I'll come and check on you in a few minutes.'

'Can we have sausages in the morning?' he asked.

'Yes,' I smiled. 'Of course you can. Sausages for breakfast.'

As I went downstairs to get the girls, I couldn't help but think what a sweet yet shy little lad he seemed to be.

Melodie and Poppy were still glued to the TV.

'Come on girls,' I told them. 'Your turn for a bath now.'

'I don't want no bath,' moaned Melodie, as I ushered them up the stairs. 'Baths are for babies.'

'OK, you can have a shower then,' I told her. 'I can show you how to turn it on and get you some towels.'

I got out my basket of toothbrushes and got them to pick one each.

'I've put some pyjamas on the bed for you that will do for tonight.'

Melodie picked hers up and looked at the label.

'I don't like these,' she moaned. 'They're too pink and babyish. Mum gets ours from Primark, not ASDA.'

'We can sort out some different ones tomorrow,' I told her. 'You'll just have to make do with these tonight.'

But I could see she wasn't impressed.

I'd tried to make their bedroom nice and cosy too. They had yellow and white striped duvets on each of the beds, there was a hot water bottle and a blanket on each one.

'Hopefully you'll be nice and warm tonight,' I told them. 'I'm sure you'll feel better after a good night's sleep.'

'Where's the telly?' asked Melodie. 'We like watching TV when we go to bed.'

'I'm afraid I don't have a TV up here, lovey,' I told her. 'I don't do TVs in bedrooms in this house. I've got lots of books if you want something to read?' But Melodie shook her head.

Again, I could see that neither of them was impressed.

'Where's Bobby?' asked Poppy.

'He's had a bath and he's in bed in his room,' I told her. 'Do you all share a room at home?'

Poppy nodded.

'Our flat's got two bedrooms so me and Melodie have got a bunk bed and Bobby's on his bed on the floor.'

'It might feel strange then tonight, being in your own rooms and not all in together,' I said.

'We don't care,' said Melodie. 'We don't want him in our room. Mum's put in for a bigger flat to the council cos we want our own bedroom and not to have to be in with Bobby cos he wets the bed.'

Poppy sniggered.

'Your brother can't help it,' I told them.

'I told you he ain't our real brother,' Melodie said impatiently. 'He's got his own dad.'

While Poppy had her shower, I went to check on Bobby as I hadn't heard a peep from him. I popped my head around his door.

'Oh sweetheart,' I whispered.

He was still sat up in bed with a book open on his lap but his eyes were closed and he was fast asleep.

I gently put the book back on the bedside table and carefully moved him down into the bed and pulled the duvet over him.

'Night night, lovey,' I whispered.

He was in such a deep sleep, he didn't even stir. I left the night light on in the corner and stood by his bed for a minute.

None of us were sure what had happened or what was going on at home, but he seemed such a shy, delicate little thing.

Meanwhile, the girls had both managed to have a shower and get themselves into the pyjamas that I'd left out for them.

I saw the clippers on the side and suddenly remembered their nails. But when I looked at both girls' feet, they were absolutely fine. Unlike Bobby's, their nails were short and clean.

Finally, I managed to get them both into bed. The girls slept in the same beds as they did at home – Melodie on the top bunk and Poppy on the bottom.

'Night girls,' I said. 'I hope you sleep well. I'll just be downstairs if you need anything and my bedroom's just down the hallway.'

They'd both gone very quiet now and I could see that they were shattered.

'I know it's hard but we'll find out more tomorrow,' I told them.

Melodie rolled over in the top bunk so she had her back to me.

Poppy nodded sadly.

I closed their door, leaving a little gap so they could see the landing light, then I went downstairs.

While they hopefully drifted off to sleep, I still had work to do.

I put all the clothes they'd come in into the washing machine. Then I went through my cupboards to see if I'd got the basics for them in the right sizes. Whenever any of the supermarkets had a sale on, I'd buy multi-packs of pants and socks and I always picked up things like jeans, T-shirts and jumpers. After a quick rifle through, I realised that there was enough to cobble an outfit together for each of them for the following day. We'd definitely need a shopping trip at some point though.

In the hallway, at the bottom of the stairs, were the school bags that the children had brought with them. The girls had got matching purple rucksacks. In each one was a pencil case, a water bottle, a reading book and a PE kit. It was in stark contrast to the tatty supermarket carrier bag that Bobby had arrived with. Inside his carrier bag was just a dog-eared reading book and nothing else. It was very odd that everything of the girls had looked good quality and new, whereas Bobby's stuff was tatty and worn.

I put the kettle on and made myself a cup of tea. Every evening I had to do what was called my daily recordings. These were my notes about that day, what had happened with each child, what they had said and done and anything else of note. Then I had to send them to Becky, my supervising social worker, and Patsy, the children's social worker, as well as to my fostering agency. There was always a lot to write up on the first day: how the children had arrived, my first impressions of them, anything they had said or done of note, how they seemed. It was good to get it all down while it was still fresh in my mind. I took a swig of tea and started to tap away on my laptop. I had a long night ahead of me.

FOUR

Secrets and Sausages

The smell of sausages wafted through the air as I glanced at the clock on the kitchen wall.

It had gone nine o'clock and the children were still in bed. I'd set my alarm for seven to make sure that I was up before them but, so far, all was quiet.

You never knew how children were going to sleep on their first night in a strange house but thankfully I hadn't heard a peep from any of them. I, on the other hand, had been on high alert, listening out for any noise or sign that they were upset or unsettled. By the time it had got light, I was already showered, dressed and sitting downstairs with a cup of tea, watching the sunrise through the patio doors that overlooked my garden.

I was keeping my promise to Bobby and making us all sausage sandwiches for breakfast. I decided to cook them and keep them warm in the oven while I went to wake the children up. But as I was setting the table, I heard the floor creaking above me.

Someone was up.

I turned the grill off and went upstairs. Bobby was standing on the landing, looking groggy. The age-seven pyjamas hung off his frail body and once again I was struck by how delicate he looked.

'Morning,' I smiled. 'You've had a good sleep.'

He gave me a confused look.

'Can you remember my name?' I asked him.

He shook his head shyly.

'I'm Maggie,' I said. 'Remember Patsy brought you to my house last night?'

He nodded.

Young children will often wake up upset and confused on their first day in the care system. Everything is so unfamiliar and it often takes them a while to realise where they are. It's as if their brain blocks things out that are too much for them to cope with. You can tell them your name the night before but often they won't remember it so I always try to remind them. It's always heartbreaking when a child wakes up crying but all you can do is try to comfort them. Thankfully Bobby seemed more confused than upset.

'Why don't you go down to the kitchen and I'll go and get your sisters up?' I suggested. 'I don't think they're awake yet.'

Bobby hesitated at the top of the stairs.

'Don't worry, flower, I'll come down with you,' I told him gently. 'Just so you know where you're going.'

He followed me down the stairs and I got him sat down at the table with a beaker of orange juice.

'It smells nice,' he said in a quiet voice.

'That's the sausages I've been cooking for your breakfast,' I smiled. 'I've done three each. Do you think you can fit three in your tummy?'

He nodded.

'I really like sausages,' he told me. 'So I think I can eat lots.'

It was lovely to hear his voice as he'd hardly said a word last night.

'I'm just going to go and wake up the girls then I'll get the sausages out,' I told him. 'I'll be back down in a couple of minutes. Is that OK?'

He nodded.

I went back upstairs to the larger bedroom where the girls were sleeping. They were both lying in bed but I could see that they were awake.

'Good morning girls, are you ready for breakfast?' I said cheerily. 'Do you remember that I'm Maggie and you came here last night with your social worker?' I added.

'Yeah, we're not stupid,' scowled Melodie.

'Are we going home today?' asked Poppy

'I'm not sure, flower, until I speak to your social worker Patsy,' I told her. 'Anyway, your brother's just woken up and he's downstairs so let's go and join him for breakfast.'

'I keep telling you, he ain't our brother,' snapped Melodie.

'Come on,' I said, quickly changing the subject. 'You must both be starving.'

I handed them a dressing gown each to put on and they followed me down the stairs. As soon as we walked into the kitchen, Bobby lowered his head and stared at the floor.

'Who's ready for sausage sandwiches?' I asked.

Bobby gave a little nod.

'I don't like sausages,' said Melodie.

'Well you can have some cereal instead then,' I told her. 'I've got lots of different kinds so you can pick your favourite.'

I put all of the boxes on the table as well as some milk. Then I gave everyone else a sausage sandwich.

Just like the night before, Bobby tucked in hungrily.

'Are we going home today?' asked Poppy again.

'Like I said before, I'm afraid I don't know right now,' I explained. 'I know you're not going to school today but I need to speak to Patsy, your social worker, and find out what's happening.'

'But if we're not going to school then what are we doing?' asked Melodie, as she tucked into a bowl of Crunchy Nut Cornflakes.

'We need to go to the shops and get you all some clothes,' I said.

'But we've got our clothes at home,' said Poppy.

'I think Patsy went round to speak to your parents yesterday but she wasn't able to talk to them properly or get any clothes for you,' I explained. 'Hopefully she'll be able to do that today but just in case, we'll get you all a few bits to tide you over.'

The girls just looked confused and Bobby didn't say a word.

After breakfast, I laid out the clothes that I'd found for them in my cupboards on their beds.

The girls weren't happy.

'I ain't wearing this,' said Melodie, turning her nose up at the jeans and sweatshirt that I'd left out.

'It's just for today and you can choose some clothes at the supermarket this morning,' I told her.

'But I don't like it,' she complained. 'I want my own clothes from home.'

'I'm afraid that's not possible at the moment,' I told her.

'This is all your fault,' she said, frowning at Bobby, who was lingering in the doorway. 'Stupid liar.'

As Melodie turned to him, it was almost as if I could see him shrink into himself. He pressed his body against the door frame, almost like he was trying to make himself invisible.

'The decision to take you into care was Social Services',' I told her firmly. 'It's about keeping you all safe. You can talk to Patsy about it later when she comes round but it isn't anybody's fault.'

Melodie didn't say anything else but I wasn't convinced that she truly believed what I was saying. I was struck by the fact that the girls were constantly asking about going home to their mum but Bobby hadn't mentioned his parents once.

I took Bobby to his room and got some clothes out for him.

'Are you OK to put these on, poppet, or would you like me to help you?'

'I'm OK,' he nodded.

While he got changed, I made his bed and tidied up some things around him. He went to take his pyjama top off and as he pulled it over his shoulders, I noticed him wince.

'Are those bruises a little bit sore?' I asked.

He nodded.

'I think I've got some special cream downstairs that will help them to heal so remind me to put some on later, OK?'

'Thanks,' he said.

Even though I was curious and this would have been an ideal time to ask him about the bruises, I knew that I couldn't. It wasn't my place as a foster carer to ask those kind of questions when a police and Social Services investigation was ongoing. If Bobby had volunteered any information, then that would be different, but he hadn't. At this early stage, you had to be careful not to be seen as prompting children or putting words into their mouths.

I left Bobby to it while I went to check on the girls. They were both dressed.

'Bobby's still getting ready,' I told them. 'So how about you two do some drawing downstairs.'

'I love drawing,' said Poppy although Melodie didn't look very interested.

I took them down to the kitchen and got out a pile of paper and a pot of felt tips and coloured pencils.

'How about you do a drawing of your family?' I suggested. They both nodded. 'It would really help me to know who's who because I keep getting it wrong, don't I?'

When I went back upstairs, Bobby was dressed and was flicking through some books.

'Good boy,' I told him. 'Give your teeth a brush now and then you're all done.'

When we came back down again, the girls were sitting at the table.

'We've done you a picture,' said Melodie.

I picked up the piece of paper. To the left were three figures. They all had long, flowing dark hair and were wearing pink and purple dresses and high heels.

'That's us and our mummy,' said Poppy.

Then right across the other side of the paper, on the right, were two stick figures. They looked hastily drawn and didn't have any features on them or clothes.

'That's him and his dad,' said Melodie, gesturing to Bobby.

'And is Bobby's dad your mummy's husband?' I asked.

'No,' said Melodie quickly. 'He's her boyfriend.'

'And what's his name?' I asked.

'Lee,' said Bobby quietly. 'My daddy's called Lee.'

There was also another figure on the picture, high up at the top of the page above all of the other people. I thought perhaps it might be a grandparent or someone in the family who had died.

'And who's this up here?' I asked.

'That's our dad,' said Poppy. 'He lives a long way away. But that's not *his* dad,' she added, gesturing to Bobby again. 'And he hasn't got a mum.'

'No,' sniggered Melodie. 'She probably didn't want him.'

'Melodie, I'd appreciate it if you'd keep your thoughts to yourself,' I told her firmly. 'I doubt that you've ever met Bobby's mum so you don't know.'

Bobby didn't say a word. Any time the girls were around, he went deathly quiet.

I kept the piece of paper safe so I could show it to Patsy.

Strangely, just as I was thinking about her, she rang my mobile.

'How are the children?' she asked. 'Did they sleep OK? When can I pop round?'

'They're doing fine,' I told her. 'Actually we're just about to go out to the shops to get them a few things. But we'll be back about midday. Is that OK?'

'That's good for me,' she replied.

I quickly wandered out of the kitchen and into the hall so I wasn't within earshot of the children.

'Have you managed to get hold of Mum and Dad?' I asked Patsy.

'I'm just about to go round there now,' she told me. 'So I'll let you know how it goes.'

After I'd hung up, I got the kids rounded up and into the car and we headed to the supermarket.

First of all, I got them to show me what food they liked. As always, the girls dominated the conversation, telling me how they went to the supermarket with their mum and what they liked.

'And what about you, Bobby?' I asked him. 'What are your favourites?'

'I like sausages,' he said, giving me a little smile.

'I will make sure I've got some more of those in our trolley,' I told him. 'What else do you like to eat?' I asked him but he struggled to tell me.

After we'd got some food, we headed over to the clothes section. I got them all a packet of underwear, socks and another pair of pyjamas.

I didn't draw attention to it but I'd also put a pair of school trousers into the trolley for Bobby as the pair he had arrived in were so tatty.

I got them each to choose some jeans or leggings and a couple of tops.

The girls took ages.

'I don't like any of these ones,' grumbled Melodie.

'We don't need clothes if we're going home,' Poppy added.

'These are just to tide you over until we know more about what's happening,' I told them again. 'And when you do go home, you can take them with you.'

When we went over to the boys' section, I could see Bobby was struggling to choose anything.

'Hurry up, Bobby,' sighed Poppy.

'He doesn't deserve new stuff cos he ruins everything,' said Melodie.

'Well it's not your decision and as I'm buying them, everybody gets new clothes today,' I told her.

I was shocked at how cruel she could be to Bobby.

'What about this one, lovey?' I asked, holding up a blue sweatshirt with a Formula One car on the front.

'OK,' he shrugged.

I chose that one and a plain green top and two pairs of jeans.

'Right, I think we're done,' I smiled.

Back at home, I put the TV on while I unpacked the shopping and got some lunch ready. I also had one eye on the clock as I knew Patsy was coming round at midday.

I hoped there would be some developments to report. I remembered Patsy was a stickler for being on time, which I liked because I was the same myself. Sure enough, bang on 12 p.m., there was a knock at the door.

The children were still in the living room, engrossed in the TV.

When she came in, she popped her head around the door to the living room. 'Hello kids, I'm just going to speak to Maggie for a minute then I'll come and chat to you all,' she told them.

None of them said a word or even looked up at her in recognition.

'Come through to the kitchen and I'll make us a coffee,' I told her. 'It's chilly out there.'

'It really is,' she said.

As I poured hot water into two mugs and added the coffee, we chatted.

'So, how did it go with the parents?' I asked.

'Well, I went with a police officer and that certainly made the difference,' she said. 'We saw mum – Brianna – but Dad was at work unfortunately.'

Patsy explained that she still wouldn't let them into the flat and had refused to give her any clothes for the children.

'So the officer said he had no option but to question them down at the police station if they weren't willing to cooperate.'

He had explained to her that they were being questioned on suspicion of assault. He told her that she needed to phone her partner and they both needed to attend the local police station to be interviewed.

'If they failed to attend, they would be under arrest.'

'How did Mum react to that?'

'As you'd imagine, she wasn't very happy,' Patsy told me. 'She was shouting and swearing.'

'What's going to happen now then?' I asked her.

'For now, both parents are being questioned so we'll see what comes of that,' she told me. 'The police have my details so they're going to let me know. For now, the children will stay in the care system.'

She explained that the EPO was valid for seven days.

'If the parents cooperate then we could look at transferring that to a Section 20. If they don't then we'll have no option but to take out an interim care order. At this stage, it looks like we're going to have to do a bit more digging.'

I nodded.

'I've been doing a bit of digging of my own,' I told her.

I showed her the picture that Melodie and Poppy had drawn.

'Yes, that makes sense from what limited information Mum gave us and what the school said,' she nodded.

She confirmed that the two girls were Brianna's from a previous relationship.

'The girls said their dad lives a long way away and they don't see him very often,' I told her.

'That's something we definitely need to look into as we'll need to contact him,' she said.

Even though the girls didn't see him, if Social Services were going to go for a care order at some stage, their biological dad would need to be informed about the proceedings.

'Lee is Bobby's biological dad and he and Brianna got together a couple of years ago,' she said.

'The girls said Bobby's mum isn't around?' I asked.

'That's right,' nodded Patsy. 'I'm not sure of the exact circumstances yet but I don't think she's been in his life since he was a baby. Lee has largely been a single dad until he and Brianna got together.'

No one had even met Lee yet and the children's school hadn't had any contact with him.

'As frustrating as it is, I think we need to sit tight on this one as we don't have any answers just now,' Patsy told me.

'The girls are going to be cross,' I replied. 'They're constantly asking when they can go home to Mum.'

'What about Bobby?' she asked.

'He's not said a thing,' I told her. 'He's not mentioned Mum or Dad.'

I explained how my first impressions were that the children were very different.

'There's definitely a divide there,' I said. 'Bobby practically shrinks into himself when the girls are around and he goes silent. The girls are very self-assured in comparison.'

'You do often get very different characters within family units,' nodded Patsy. 'Especially blended families.'

But I couldn't help thinking that there was much much more to this family – there was so much that we didn't know. But we had to be patient and, gradually, the truth would reveal itself.

FIVE

Questions Not Answers

Now we needed to tell the children what was happening.

Patsy wasn't going to let them know that the police were involved and that they were questioning both parents on suspicion of assault, but we needed to explain that they were going to be staying with me a little while longer.

'If Mum and Dad continue to refuse to cooperate then we don't know how long it's going to take,' said Patsy. 'So let's try and get them back to some sort of normality and take them to school tomorrow.'

'OK,' I said.

I explained that I could do with some more pieces of Bobby's uniform.

'I picked up some trousers for him today but some jumpers and tops would be good, and a couple of extras for the girls.'

'I'm sure the school can provide you with some,' Patsy told me. 'I'm in touch with them so I'll let them know they're returning tomorrow and that you'll give them a call. Right, let's go and tell the kids.'

Patsy and I went into the living room and I turned the TV off. Melodie and Poppy looked at Patsy expectantly, while Bobby stared at the floor.

'Are we going home?' asked Poppy.

'I'm afraid not,' said Patsy. 'We're still talking to your parents so, for now, you're going to be staying here with Maggie.'

'But that's not fair,' sighed Poppy with tears in her eyes.

And I could see from Melodie's expression that she was furious.

'He's a liar,' she spat, pointing at Bobby. 'He's stupid and a waste of space and he makes things up just to get attention.'

Bobby jumped up off the chair and ran out of the room.

'I'll go after him,' I told Patsy.

Bobby was in the kitchen, curled up in a ball by the patio doors, sobbing.

'Hey, what's all this?' I said gently, sitting down on the floor next to him.

'Everybody hates me,' he cried. 'I'm bad and useless.'

'No, they don't,' I told him, putting a reassuring arm around him. 'You're not bad or useless – the girls are just sad that they're not allowed to go home so they're just looking for someone to blame . . . I know you must be sad too not to see Mummy and Daddy.'

'She isn't my mummy,' he said, wiping his nose. 'She's Brianna.'

'Gosh, I keep getting it wrong, don't I?' I sighed. 'I am so sorry.'

I rubbed his back.

'None of this is your fault,' I told him.

Just then, Patsy came into the kitchen to find us.

'I'm sorry that Melodie was mean to you, Bobby,' she said. 'I've explained to her that everyone will have different feelings about what's happening, but there's no need for her to lash out just because she's feeling angry and upset.'

He looked up at her with his bloodshot blue eyes and nodded.

'The girls are upset that they're not going home and it must be very strange and unsettling for all of you,' she told him. 'But we need to get to the bottom of how you got those bruises first, Bobby, so I'm going to have to ask you some questions about that.'

Bobby looked down at the floor and didn't say a word.

'Come on,' I told him gently. 'Let's go back into the living room.'

Neither of the girls said anything when we walked back in.

'So tomorrow we think it's a good idea for you all to go back to school,' Patsy told them.

'Will Mum take us?' asked Poppy hopefully.

'Maggie will take you in the morning and pick you up tomorrow afternoon,' Patsy told her. 'And then later in the week we'll try and arrange for you to see your parents at a contact centre after school.'

They all looked puzzled.

'What's that?' asked Poppy.

'Contact centres are special buildings where parents can meet with their children. There are books and toys there and you can have a drink, play a game and just spend time with your mummy and daddy.'

'Why can't we just go to our flat and see them?' asked Melodie.

'Well, sometimes we need somebody else to be there to make sure that everybody is safe,' Patsy explained.

'Safe, safe, safe,' she spat. 'Why do you keep saying that word? We *are* safe.'

'It's not just about you, Melodie, it's about everyone being safe,' she told her. 'Bobby's got some marks on his body and we need to make sure that he's being kept safe too.'

'Well, he should be good then,' mumbled Melodie.

'What do you mean by that?' Patsy asked her.

'Nothing,' she sighed.

But it was an odd thing to say.

There was nothing more Patsy could say and she had to get back to the office for a meeting.

'I'll be in touch when I hear from the police,' she told me as I walked her to the front door.

That afternoon, I was determined to get the kids out of the house so I took them to the park. It was freezing cold but I think we all needed some fresh air. The girls weren't interested in playing in the playground but we walked around the lake and I bought us all a hot chocolate, which stopped the moaning for a while.

I was just putting the tea on when Patsy phoned.

'Both parents have been released without charge,' she told me.

'What did they say?' I asked.

'They denied everything,' she told me. 'Mum is still insistent Bobby is a difficult child and likes to cause problems by making things up. She says the bruises probably happened when he was play-fighting at school.'

I was also intrigued to hear more about Bobby's dad, Lee.

'He hardly said a word apparently,' she said. 'Refused to answer any questions about his son.'

It was all so frustrating. Without any concrete evidence, the police couldn't prove a crime had been committed or charge anyone. But at the same time, Social Services couldn't let the children return home either.

'Could the bruises have happened when he was playing?' I asked Patsy.

'The police are sure they were caused by adult-sized fingers – like someone was grabbing him. Plus there are the older, faded bruises on his back that no one has an adequate explanation for either. It's unlikely that another child could grab him with such force to cause marks like that.'

I wasn't sure what was going to happen now.

'The only person who knows the truth and is most likely to tell us is Bobby,' Patsy told me. 'So the police would like to speak to him as soon as possible.'

When the girls went to school the following morning, Patsy wanted me to bring Bobby to the police station to be interviewed. It worried me how he was going to cope with that.

'It will be handled sensitively, won't it?' I asked. 'As you saw today, he's a fragile little soul.'

'Of course,' replied Patsy. 'We don't even have to tell him it's the police. He'll be interviewed by a non-uniformed officer in a special interview suite at the station and I will be there with him.'

Many larger police stations had a special room or suite where children, witnesses to crimes or vulnerable people could be spoken to or interviewed. These sorts of rooms were often used for victims of sexual assaults or bereaved families too.

Once I'd made arrangements with Patsy, I went to tell the children.

'We still need to find out how Bobby's arms got bruised,' I told them. 'So tomorrow, Bobby, while the girls are at school, we're going to go and see some people whose job it is to talk to children to find out how they've been hurt.'

'Don't they want to speak to us?' asked Poppy.

'Not just yet, lovey,' I told her. 'Only Bobby to begin with.'

Even though I'd tried not to make a big deal of it, I could see Bobby was apprehensive.

'Are the people we'll see tomorrow nice?' he asked me when I tucked him into bed that night. 'Or are they mean?'

'They are very nice,' I reassured him. 'You just need to tell them the truth and if you don't know the answer to a question then just tell them that. They just want to make sure that you're OK.

'You never know, we might have time to stop for a hot chocolate somewhere on the way back,' I added and he gave me a little smile.

I understood how he felt; I was apprehensive too. It was never nice taking children to a police station to be interviewed. Even though they tried to make it as relaxed and comfortable as possible, it was still scary for a child going into a noisy, busy police station. It was intimidating for me as an adult.

I hardly slept a wink that night as I went over the plan for the following day in my mind. I knew I had to get the girls to school which was a forty-five-minute drive away from my house and then Bobby and I had to be at the police station. I was worried about how he was going to cope with it all.

Thankfully, the girls seemed happy to be going to school.

'Bobby and I will come in with you,' I told them, as we pulled up outside the school the next day.

'Do you have to?' sighed Melodie. 'We know where our classrooms are.'

'I want to come and introduce myself to your teachers,' I added firmly.

Bobby hung back while I quickly said hello to Poppy's Year Five teacher, Mr Bland.

'I'm a foster carer, and Melodie and Poppy are going to be staying with me for a little while,' I explained. 'I've left my details at the office so if you ever need to speak to me then please do give me a ring.'

I said the same to Melodie's teacher, Ms Rice, who was head of Year Six. They'd already met Patsy the day that the head teacher had called Social Services.

It took longer than I expected and Bobby and I were running late by the time we got back into the car. He'd been very quiet all morning.

'How are you doing?' I asked him and he shrugged.

'Don't be nervous. Patsy will be there too and you can show her your lovely new racing car top.'

Bobby looked down at his jumper as if to remind himself of what he was wearing.

I'd never been to this particular police station before so it was a surprise to pull up outside a huge modern building. It was the complete opposite to most of the dilapidated old police stations that I'd been to before. It was normally polystyrene ceilings and peeling walls but this was all glass and gleaming steel.

Patsy was waiting for us in the car park.

'There's absolutely nothing to worry about, Bobby,' she said to him.

But as we walked through the entrance into a huge reception area, I felt his little hand tightly grip my arm. The room was crammed full of people. Some were slumped on plastic chairs, others were talking noisily on mobile phones.

I could see Bobby was intrigued.

'Why are there so many policemen here?' he asked.

'Oh, the special place that we need to go to is at the back of the police station,' I told him. 'It won't be as noisy there.'

Patsy went to the front desk and a few minutes later, a woman came out from behind the perspex screen and then she and Patsy walked over to us.

She was wearing a white shirt and black trousers and had long red hair and a friendly face.

'This is DC Liz Orton,' Patsy told me.

She bent down to Bobby so she was at his level.

'Hello young man,' she smiled. 'I'm Liz. Let's go and find my comfy room. It's nice and cosy and I'm sure I've got some biscuits in there. Do you like biscuits?'

Bobby nodded. Then he looked up at me and I gave him a reassuring smile.

'Are you coming to get a biscuit too?' he asked me.

It wouldn't normally be procedure for a foster carer to accompany a child into a police interview. I looked at Patsy.

'Would you like Maggie to come with you?' Patsy asked Bobby and he nodded.

'I'm happy for Maggie to come into the interview room with us while we show Bobby around and get him settled,' suggested Liz.

'Thank you,' I said. 'I appreciate that.'

I'd only met Bobby thirty-six hours ago but I was happy I could help to bring him some comfort during such a hard time.

We followed Liz down a rabbit warren of corridors until we got to a large black door.

'Wow,' I said, as she pushed it open and we walked in.

It was the nicest interview room that I'd ever seen. These sorts of rooms were normally run down with second-hand worn furniture and tatty books and toys. This one had a big squishy sofa and two chairs, a big bright yellow rug and the walls were painted a lovely blue.

'There's a big shelf of books over there,' Liz showed Bobby. 'And lots of toys.'

There were some monster trucks and cars already set out on the coffee table, which he went over to straight away.

'Bobby, would you like a carton of apple juice and a biscuit?'

He nodded eagerly.

'Cup of tea?' she asked us, and we both nodded.

I knew they were always overstretched and busy and I really appreciated the way that she was trying to make Bobby feel at home and not rush into asking him questions straight away.

As Liz made tea in the little kitchenette in the corner, I looked around. Even though the room was bright and welcoming, there were still signs of what its true purpose was. There were cameras on the walls in all four corners of the room which I knew was so they could catch all of a child's expressions, no matter which way they were facing.

There was also a side room. The door was open and I could see there was a toilet and a shower in there. I knew these types of rooms were there in case people needed to be medically examined.

Even though it was just an informal chat with Bobby, it would still be videoed in case it needed to be used for evidence further down the line. They also didn't like to have to put children through interviews too many times.

Bobby seemed OK as he sipped on his juice and munched his biscuit while looking cautiously at the toys.

'You can sit on the floor and play with those if you like,' Patsy told him.

He sat down on the rug next to the coffee table and Liz came and sat on the sofa near him.

'I'm really lucky, Bobby, because my job is to talk to children like you,' she told him. 'Would it be OK to chat to you?'

He nodded.

'I'll try and listen really carefully but sometimes I might forget things so I like to make a video to help me remember. Can you see the cameras up there?'

Bobby looked up to where she was pointing.

'They are going to record us so we can remember what we were all talking about.'

Even though they were children, police still had to make them aware that they were being filmed. Bobby seemed intrigued by it more than anything.

'So, Bobby, I'm going to ask you a few questions now,' Liz told him gently.

I took that as my queue to leave. I grabbed my bag and got up.

'Bobby, I'll be right outside having my cup of tea and I'll see you when you come out,' I told him.

'No, no, no,' he said, suddenly panicked. 'Don't go.'

He got up and ran over to me.

'You're OK, sweetie,' I told him. 'Patsy and Liz will be with you and I'll be right outside.'

'No, please stay,' he begged, throwing his arms around my waist.

'Flower, I'm not allowed to,' I replied.

I didn't want to risk jeopardising the interview in any way or somehow make it inadmissible to the courts if it got that far. You had to be so careful not to be seen as influencing a child or their answers.

'Maggie, I'm happy for you to sit in on the interview,' said Liz. 'It's clear Bobby would be more comfortable with you here.'

'OK, thank you,' I said.

I moved off the sofa to one of the seats that was behind Bobby so he knew I was there but I wasn't making direct eye contact with him.

As Liz started chatting to him, Bobby began to play with the toy trucks.

'So, Bobby, tell me who lives in your house,' she asked him.

'Melodie, Poppy, Daddy and Brianna,' he said matter-of-factly.

Then she got him to tell her who everyone was.

'Do you like to play with Melodie and Poppy?' she asked. He shrugged.

'What kind of toys or games do you like to play with at home?'

Bobby shrugged again.

'What do you like to eat for your breakfast?'

Bobby turned round and looked at me and smiled.

'Sausage sandwiches,' he said.

'Yes, we had those yesterday morning, didn't we?' I said and he nodded.

'Do you have sausage sandwiches for breakfast at home?' Liz asked him.

'No,' he said, spinning round the wheels on one of the trucks.

I could see Liz was doing her best to make him comfortable and get him relaxed but whenever she asked him a question about his family, he seemed to clam up.

'Can you remember how you got those bruises on your arms, Bobby?' Liz asked him.

Bobby got the two monster trucks and bashed them together.

'Crash!' he said. 'Bang!'

'Did they happen at home?' she asked him.

'Smash,' he said, pushing the trucks off the coffee table onto the floor.

I could see he was doing everything he could to avoid answering Liz's questions.

'Those trucks look like really good fun,' smiled Liz. 'Can I play too?'

Bobby shrugged.

Liz got off her chair and sat on the floor next to him.

'This one's a monster truck,' she said, picking one up. 'I can tell by the size of its wheels.'

For the next few minutes, she played with the trucks alongside Bobby, who was eyeing her suspiciously.

'Was Daddy there when you got hurt?' she asked.

'Bash, boom,' he yelled. 'Oh no, the trucks have had a crash.'

'And where was Mummy?'

'She's not my mummy, she's Brianna,' he said firmly.

'Where was Brianna when you got hurt?' she repeated.

'These trucks have very big wheels,' he said.

'You're right,' smiled Liz. 'I think they're monster trucks as well.'

She paused.

'Did you get hurt at home, Bobby?' she asked him.

'I think the wheels on your truck are the biggest,' he told her.

It didn't matter what Liz asked; if it was anything about his family then Bobby ignored her and deflected the conversation back to the toy trucks.

Liz looked at Patsy and she shrugged.

There wasn't a lot anyone could do. If Bobby didn't want to answer her questions then nobody could make him. It was frustrating but all they could do was leave it for now and perhaps try to talk to Bobby another day.

'Well thank you for chatting to me, Bobby,' Liz told him, getting up off the floor 'It's been really nice to meet you. Will you come back if I want to talk to you again?'

'Will the trucks still be here?' he asked.

'Yes, of course,' she replied and Bobby nodded.

Then he got up and came over to me.

'Can we go now?' he asked.

Patsy walked out with us to the car park.

'You did so well, Bobby,' said Patsy encouragingly. 'I know Liz was asking you a lot of things.'

I knew neither of us wanted him to feel like he had failed or let us down.

'That wasn't too bad, was it?' I smiled. 'Shall we go and find somewhere on the way home to get a hot chocolate?'

'I liked those trucks,' he replied. 'Have you got trucks at your house?'

'I think I might in my loft,' I told him. 'I'll have a look this afternoon and try to dig them out for you.'

I didn't want him to feel bad, but really we were no further forward in finding out the truth. Bobby wasn't saying anything and neither were his parents. We were at a stalemate.

The consensus of all the professionals seemed to be that Bobby's bruises weren't accidental. Someone must have hurt him, but how on earth did we get him to tell us who?

SIX

Close Contact

It had felt like a long day. When Patsy called me that evening, I could hear the frustration in her voice too.

'So far, the police haven't got any evidence that could lead to a prosecution or, in fact, any evidence that a crime has been committed,' she told me. 'But from Social Service's point of view, I've spoken to my manager and we feel that we need to do further investigation.'

Patsy had called Brianna and Lee earlier.

'I was very clear that we needed both of them to start engaging with us,' she told me. 'And I explained that until they did, their children would not be returning home and would be remaining in the care system until we carried out further investigations.'

One fact in all of this hadn't changed: a child had unexplained bruising. I understood that Social Services could only let the children go back home if they were sure there had been no foul play and the kids would be safe.

'How did they react to that?' I asked.

'Well, it was Brianna who answered and she wasn't very happy,' she told me.

I knew from experience that what would happen now was evidence-gathering. Social Services would talk to the children's school, and any other adults they came into contact with, and start to build up a picture of their lives. Patsy was also going to get in touch with the girls' biological father and inform him of what was happening.

'I'd also like to start contact sessions this week,' said Patsy.

That would also help Social Services to see both parents with the children and see how they all interacted.

'What are you thinking?' I asked her.

'An hour after school twice a week?' she suggested.

Babies and younger children who didn't have school would sometimes see their parents once a day, or every couple of days. But when children had school, it was generally twice a week.

Contact would be supervised and it would take place in a contact centre, run by Social Services designed for parents and their children to spend time together while they were supervised by a contact worker. They had kitchens and bathrooms so parents could make meals for their children and, if they were babies, give them a bath, and sometimes they had gardens. They were neutral, safe spaces designed to replicate a home environment.

'I'll find out which centres have availability and let you know ASAP,' Patsy said.

There was a variety of centres scattered around the county but demand was so great, it often took a while to find a contact centre with available space on a regular basis. For continuity's sake, they tried to organise all of the sessions at the same centre on the same days and times each week.

Social Services would also have to decide what they were going to do about care orders. The children were currently on an EPO that lasted seven days. The easiest way forward was for the parents to agree to a Section 20. If they weren't willing to do that, then Social Services could apply to the courts for an interim care order, which would give the local authority parental responsibility for all three children.

Fortunately Patsy quickly found a contact centre with space so I told the children about it the following evening.

'Patsy's arranged for you to see your mummy and daddy after school tomorrow,' I told them. 'It will be at a contact centre like we talked about the other day.'

I made sure that when I said 'Mummy' I looked at the girls and that when I said Daddy I looked at Bobby as I knew how annoyed Melodie got when I referred to Lee as their dad.

'But what will we do there again?' asked Poppy.

'You'll be able to see your mum and Lee and play a game or do some drawing or just chat and spend some time with them.'

The girls seemed excited about seeing their mum but throughout all of this conversation, Bobby hadn't said a word.

I hadn't been to this centre before so I wasn't sure what to expect. It was in the area near where the children lived and over an hour's drive away from my house.

I picked the children up after school and I'd got a snack ready for them to have in the car; I knew they'd already be tired after school and I didn't want them to be hungry as well. I knew this was already going to be emotionally draining for them.

However, as we left school, the traffic was terrible.

'Come on,' I muttered to myself as I sat in the traffic jam.

The ideal scenario, and one most social workers favour, is for the children to arrive first so they are already settled in the contact room by the time their parents get there. This way, the social worker can show them around the contact centre, answer any questions and get them as comfortable as possible. It also works best for foster carers as it means we can normally leave or be out of the way so I don't have to be introduced to birth parents, which can often be awkward or upsetting for them.

However, the traffic was so bad, we were fifteen minutes late by the time I pulled into the car park. My heart sank when I saw the contact centre. It was a run-down, drab 1960's prefab with a flat roof in the grounds of a Social Services' office. I could already tell from the state of the exterior that the interior wasn't going to be much better.

As we walked across the car park, I could see Patsy in the reception area.

'There's Mum!' shouted Poppy and my heart sank.

The girls stormed ahead and ran into the entrance while Bobby hung back with me.

A woman spun round and Poppy ran towards her. She was in her twenties and had bleached blonde hair and a full face of make-up. She was quite smartly dressed in jeans, a jumper and a cream coat with heeled boots.

'Oh my girls,' she sighed, pulling Poppy and Melodie into her arms. 'I've missed you so much.'

As he walked through the door, Brianna's attention turned straight to Bobby.

'What have you been saying to your teachers?' she shouted.

'Your dad's not happy that your lies have got us into all of this trouble.'

'Brianna!' said Patsy, interrupting her. 'Remember what I said – you need to stay off this subject. I understand that this is your first contact session but maybe I wasn't clear enough about the rules of contact. The aim of this session is to spend time with the kids, not accuse them of things. It's for you to be reassured that they're OK and for them to be reassured that you're still around.'

'Hmmph,' huffed Brianna. 'I'd know they were OK if they were back at home where they belong.'

I felt Bobby pressing himself into my leg and I patted his shoulder for reassurance.

'Bobby, your dad is here,' said Patsy gently. 'He's just at the toilet.'

A few seconds later, a man walked back into reception. He was tall and skinny with a pale, sullen face and I guessed he was in his late twenties. He had a baseball cap pulled over his face but underneath it I could see that he had a black eye. Even though it was a freezing cold day, he had a threadbare T-shirt on and his jeans were covered in holes.

'Hi Bobby,' he said quietly.

'Hi,' said Bobby, not making eye contact with him.

I'd noticed that the girls hadn't said a word to Lee.

'Gosh, Lee – is your eye OK?' Patsy asked him.

'He's been fighting again,' tutted Brianna. 'Came back from the pub like that the other night. He's always getting into trouble after a few pints, that one.'

Lee didn't say a word and just stared at his feet.

'I'm so sorry we're a bit late,' I said to Patsy quietly. 'The traffic was terrible.'

'No problem,' she told me. 'I'd best introduce you now you're here.'

So far neither Brianna nor Lee had asked who I was.

'This is Maggie,' Patsy told them. 'She's the foster carer who is currently looking after the children.'

Neither of them said a word or even acknowledged me.

Brianna was too busy asking the girls endless questions and Lee and Bobby were as silent as each other.

'Right then, shall we go through to the contact room?' suggested Patsy.

My heart sank as I peered into the drab room. It was freezing cold despite the storage heater on the wall and the windows didn't have any curtains and were dripping with condensation.

The walls were painted a garish yellow but they were patchy and dirty and the blue carpet was frayed and grubby. The only furniture in there was a tatty sofa and a chest of drawers and a bucket of plastic toys that looked like they were only good enough for the bin. The whole place looked like it could do with a good clean and renovation.

From my own experience over the years, I knew contact centres varied wildly. Some were brand spanking new while others were more like this one. I once had a contact centre that was so awful they often used to cancel sessions because the rooms were being fumigated to get rid of fleas. I was fostering an eight-month-old baby at the time and when I dropped her off there to see her mum, I used to give the contact worker a sheet to put down on the sofa before the baby was laid on it as it was so grubby.

As soon as I got her home, I'd boil wash all her clothes and the sheet. Thankfully this place didn't look that bad although I wouldn't say it was very welcoming or comfortable.

Patsy introduced Brianna and Lee to their contact worker – a woman in her forties called Palvi. As it was the first session, Patsy would stay in there for a while to check everyone was OK. As a foster carer, I wasn't really supposed to be in there so I made my excuses and left.

An hour wasn't really enough time for me to go anywhere, so I made myself a coffee in the kitchen. Then I sat in reception and messaged Louisa who had left a voicemail for me earlier that day asking how things were.

Sorry I've not been in touch, I told her. *The children are still with me so I've been busy settling them in. Still not sure what's happening but I'll see you and E soon xx*

Having lived with me for many years while I fostered other children, she understood that when I got a new placement in, it was all-consuming.

Five minutes later, the door to the contact room opened and I looked up expecting to see Patsy. Instead, Lee shuffled out. He put his head down and didn't say a word as he walked out through the front door. I could see him outside through the glass, head down, puffing on a cigarette.

He was equally silent on his way back in. Five minutes later, Patsy finally came out. She came and sat with me in reception.

'How's it going in there?' I asked her.

'OK,' she shrugged. 'It's such a strange dynamic.'

She explained that Mum and the girls had been doing all of the talking while Bobby and Lee were silent.

'I can't work it out,' she sighed. 'Bobby hasn't even said anything to Lee.'

'He's never asked about his dad or even talked about him while he's been at my house,' I told her. 'Could it be fear?'

'Who knows? It could well be. Time will tell us more. It's all very odd,' she said.

I didn't like to jump to conclusions but I got a strange vibe from Lee. He seemed a bit of a foreboding presence that everyone seemed to avoid. Did everyone ignore Lee because they were scared of him? His black eye from the pub suggested he had a violent nature.

However, as Patsy had pointed out, it was early days.

At the end of the session, the door to the contact room opened. Bobby was the first out and he quickly came over to me.

'OK lovey?' I asked him and he nodded solemnly.

I could hear the girls before I could see them – they were hysterical, clinging on to Brianna and sobbing.

'We don't want to go back to her house,' wept Poppy. 'We want to stay with you.'

'Yeah, it's horrible there and she makes us wear nasty clothes,' added Melodie.

'Don't worry my babies, you'll be home soon,' Brianna told them, giving me a dirty look. 'They know they're talking s**t. I'll make sure you get some of your nice stuff from home.'

I wasn't offended by their criticisms at all. My house wasn't the girls' home and I'd heard a lot worse from children over the years. I didn't think they had anything against me personally. If it wasn't me then it would be another foster carer and hopefully any gripes they had were against the system.

I felt Bobby pulling on my coat sleeve.

'Are we going soon?' he asked quietly.

Lee was stood over the other side of reception, kicking the empty Coke can that he'd been drinking along the floor.

He looked up and caught me staring at him then quickly looked away. I hardly knew anything about his man but from what I'd seen so far, I definitely didn't like.

SEVEN

Follow Me

Over the next few days the children and I started to settle into a routine of sorts.

People assume that you don't have much to do as a foster carer when you have school-age children. However, it was a long drive to get them to school and back, and with the few hours left in between, there was paperwork to get through and all the boring domestic stuff. Once I'd done the cleaning, the washing, the tidying and prepped dinner, I found that it was already time to go and collect the children again.

One morning, my supervising social worker, Becky, rang me for a chat.

'I just wanted to check in with you and see how things are going,' she said.

'OK,' I sighed. 'But the dynamic between the children is still puzzling me.'

I explained how the girls were very confident and vocal, but Bobby was silent and very introverted.

'It's like two extremes,' I said. 'Two rosy-cheeked,

assertive girls while their brother is pale, silent and covered in bruises.'

'Does Bobby talk to you?' asked Becky.

'He does,' I replied. 'When the girls aren't around he's a little bit more chatty, but as soon as they're in the same room, it's like he clams up.'

It was nice to talk it all through with someone.

'Remember it's early days,' Becky told me. 'Plus, as you and I both know, trauma manifests itself in different ways. Just because the girls are presenting like this doesn't mean that they are necessarily OK.'

'I know,' I said. 'It's just a feeling I get that the girls were well treated and cared for while Bobby obviously wasn't.'

I didn't want to say it out loud, but it was almost like they enjoyed talking down to Bobby and being mean to him. It seemed normal to them and they didn't seem to mind if I heard them.

'Talking to Patsy, it sounds like no one knows what the long-term plan is yet,' Becky told me.

'Yep, we just have to wait and see how the next few days and weeks play out,' I replied.

Social Services were still evidence-gathering. They were talking to Brianna and Lee, the children's school and any other adults involved in their lives. Contact was still happening twice a week, which was being supervised by Palvi, the contact worker.

One afternoon, at the end of a session, Palvi came out of the contact room with a couple of bags.

'Brianna and Lee have brought in some clothes for the children,' she told me.

'That's great,' I smiled as she handed them to me.

It was always nice for children to wear their own things and I'd had non-stop complaints from the girls about the clothes that I had given them.

It wasn't until we got home and I unloaded the bags from the car that I looked at them properly.

There was one large purple holdall and a carrier bag. I took the holdall upstairs and looked inside. Everything was neatly folded and I could tell by the smell that they'd been freshly washed. I laid everything out on my bed. There were pyjamas, leggings, jeans, jumpers and dresses for the girls; also tights, pants and a pair of trainers and shoes each. There were even two sparkly bags filled with hairclips and headbands.

But by the time I'd emptied it all out, I realised something.

It was all for the girls. There was absolutely nothing in it for Bobby.

Then I remembered the carrier bag so I ran downstairs to get it. I looked inside to find four grubby T-shirts, a couple of pairs of tracksuit bottoms and a pair of tatty trainers. They were all screwed up and felt damp and smelt of mould. There must have been a mistake. Surely that couldn't be all that they'd sent him?

I rang Patsy.

'I think there must have been a mix-up,' I told her. 'The girls have got plenty of stuff but there's no pyjamas or underwear for Bobby. In fact, he hardly has anything.'

'I'll check that Palvi hasn't got another bag,' she said.

She phoned me back ten minutes later.

'No, I'm afraid that was it,' she told me. 'That was all Brianna and Lee gave her.'

'That's so odd,' I sighed.

There seemed to be such a marked difference between the way the girls and Bobby were treated.

I took the girls' clothes to their room and started putting their things in the wardrobe.

'Oh look, Melodie, it's our stuff from home,' gasped Poppy.

'You've got some lovely things,' I said and she nodded.

'Not like Bobby,' said Melodie smugly.

'Does he not have nice things too?' I asked.

Poppy shook her head.

'He's not allowed nice things cos he just ruins them,' Melodie told me. 'He doesn't deserve nice clothes like us.'

'Well everyone has clothes at my house,' I told her.

I wasn't going to get into a discussion with a child about it.

I put the few items that Brianna and Lee had sent for Bobby through the wash to freshen them up and when they were dry I folded them up and put them in Bobby's wardrobe. I didn't want to draw his attention to the clothes, or rather the lack of them, that his parents had sent.

The children had been with me for nearly two weeks when I dropped them off at school one morning. I'd got a busy day ahead of me so when I saw a supermarket close to school, I decided to do a quick shop there on my way back home.

The car park was fairly empty so I got a space easily. As I walked towards the supermarket entrance, I noticed a small red car parked nearby. It caught my eye because it had a huge dent in the side and the wing mirror was being held on with gaffer tape; the mirror looked like it could drop off at any minute.

I was sure I'd seen the car somewhere before but I didn't think any more of it as I grabbed a trolley.

With three children in the house, I always tried to be organised and plan my meals, so I was engrossed in my shopping list as I walked up and down the aisles.

I also wanted to grab Bobby another pair of school trousers and a few other items of clothing to make up for what was lacking in the stuff that had been sent for him from home. As I was rifling through a rail of jumpers, I had a strange feeling that someone was watching me. I glanced up. There was a woman with a toddler in a buggy looking at clothes. But there, in the far corner of the kids' clothes section, was a man. He was tall with a baseball hat pulled down over his face.

There was something so familiar about him. But as I looked at him, he quickly turned around so he had his back to me and then walked off.

I phoned Patsy when I got home.

'I think I saw Lee, Bobby's dad, at the supermarket today,' I told her.

I explained how I'd popped in after dropping the kids off at school.

'Well, their flat is close by so it's not surprising,' she replied. 'Did he say anything to you or approach you?'

'No, not at all,' I said. 'I felt someone watching me but when I looked at him, he walked off.'

'He was probably just as surprised to see you,' Patsy told me.

'Yes, I think you're right,' I replied. 'It's my own fault. I'll make sure I don't go in that supermarket again and stick to the ones nearer home as there's always a risk of bumping into him or Brianna.'

Generally, wherever possible, I would try and stay out of an area where I knew birth parents lived. It definitely wouldn't have been something I would have done if the children were with me as it would be potentially distressing and unsettling bumping into their birth parents.

I didn't think any more of it but I made a mental note to be more careful in the future. The next few days passed by in the usual blur of driving to and from school and trying to cram in as many jobs as I could in between. On the way home one morning, I had a dentist's appointment. As I was walking back to my car, I noticed a red car parked close to mine.

That's funny, I thought to myself as I looked at the bashed up side and the wing mirror secured with gaffer tape – it was the same car that I'd seen in the supermarket near the children's school the previous week.

A couple of days later, I was coming out of the local post office when I saw the car again. This time it was parked on the other side of the road.

It was only when I was leaving contact a few days later that the penny finally dropped. While the children had had their session, I'd sat in reception doing some emails.

When they came out, Melodie was complaining about being hungry.

'We'll head back now. I've got a chicken casserole in the slow cooker for tea,' I told her.

'I don't like casserole,' she replied sulkily.

She carried on moaning but I got all three of them in the car and finally we were about to head home.

I'd just put on my seatbelt and was looking into the rear-view mirror when I saw Brianna and Lee leaving the contact centre. As I reversed out, I glanced over to the far corner of the car park where they were getting into their car. My chest tightened when I saw the vehicle they were getting into.

A small red car. It was the car that I'd been seeing on and off for the past few days. I knew it was the same one because of the dent in the side and the gaffer-taped wing mirror. It was always dark when we left contact and we had always left before them so I'd never noticed what car, if any, Lee and Brianna had.

It seemed too much of a coincidence and I felt sick to my stomach. When I'd seen Lee at the supermarket, had he been following me? I could explain bumping into him there but since then I'd seen his car outside the post office and the dentist the other day. All places that were at least an hour's drive away from where he and Brianna lived.

I didn't say a word to the children. As I pulled out of the contact centre, my eyes were glued to the rear-view mirror, checking to see that Lee's car wasn't behind me. I was on high alert for the whole journey with so many worst-case scenarios running through my mind. What if they followed me home? Did they want to snatch the kids?

As soon as I pulled up outside my house, I quickly got the children inside. Then I stood in the dark at my bedroom window, surveying the road. Thankfully there was no sign of the red car but it had really shaken me up.

My heart was still pounding as I got on the phone to my supervising social worker Becky.

'I think Lee's been following me,' I told her.

I explained what had happened and how I'd seen the red car all around my area for the past few days.

'Have you ever seen him in your road, Maggie?' she asked. 'Could he have followed you home from contact?'

'I don't think so,' I said. 'I checked the entire journey back and I've looked outside and I can't see anything.'

'Well, that's a relief,' she said.

If birth parents knew the address of a foster carer and it was believed that a child or children could be at risk of harm or being snatched, they would immediately have to be removed from the placement. I'd been followed home by a couple of parents in the past and I'd fostered a baby who'd had to be moved in the end because his birth parents kept turning up at my door and being abusive and threatening me. It was never a nice situation for either the children or me.

'Don't you think it seems too much of a coincidence?' I asked her.

'Maggie, I can see why it's shaken you up but Lee hasn't turned up at your house and he hasn't approached you,' she told me.

'There's nothing to say that he can't be in your part of town. For all we know, Lee could have family or friends there or he might work in the area.'

'You're right,' I sighed. 'It just felt a bit creepy somehow.'

'It's probably just a coincidence,' Becky reassured me. 'Just be vigilant and keep an eye out.'

Coincidence or not, I had a strange feeling about Lee. There was definitely something about him that made me uncomfortable. He hadn't approached me but despite what Becky had said, I was still convinced that he had been following me. But if he was, why was he doing it? I didn't think he would want to snatch the children. He and the girls didn't even acknowledge each other at contact and even with Bobby, his own biological child, there was very little interaction. Was he just playing mind games with me or trying to show me who was boss? But I knew there was no proof of anything so I tried to put it to the back of my mind.

The following morning, after I'd dropped the children off at school, I headed to Louisa's. She worked four days a week as a nanny and today was her day off. It was a good opportunity to have a cup of tea and a catch-up and see Edie.

As I walked up the stairs to her first-floor flat, I could hear Edie's little voice from behind the door. She must have watched me pull up from the window.

'Nana!'

'Yes, it's me flower!' I yelled.

As soon as Louisa opened the door, she ran into my arms.

'My goodness, you're getting so big,' I told her, covering her soft, sticky cheeks with kisses.

'Nana, baby,' she told me, grabbing my hand.

'That's her favourite game at the minute,' said Louisa. 'Playing with her baby doll 24-7. I'll go and put the kettle on while you bath and feed the baby.'

'Ooh lovely,' I laughed.

It never failed to lift my sprits coming round and seeing Louisa and my gorgeous granddaughter. I felt rather in limbo at the moment with Melodie, Poppy and Bobby. I didn't know what they'd been through, if anything, and what was going to happen to them. All of our questions still remained unanswered so in a way it was very frustrating.

'So how are you doing?' asked Louisa as she came into the living room and handed me a cup of tea.

'Oh you know, busy, I said.

'How are the kiddies getting on?' she asked.

Louisa had grown up around my fostering so she knew that for confidentiality reasons, most of the time I couldn't go into any detail about the children who were living with me or their circumstances.

'It's early days so we're still trying to work out what has gone on,' I told her.

'Are they likely to be with you for a while?' she asked.

'At this point in time, no one knows,' I shrugged. 'It's a bit of a complicated case unfortunately.'

While we were chatting, Edie was stood at the window.

'She's such a nosy neighbour,' laughed Louisa. 'She loves standing there and looking out at the road.'

'Twee,' said Edie as if on cue.

'Yes, that's right,' I told her. 'There's a tree. Can you see the leaves on it?'

Edie nodded.

'Doggy!' she laughed, pointing.

'Can you see a doggy?' I asked her. 'You love doggies, don't you?'

I put my mug down and stood up at the window with her.

'What else can you see, flower?' I asked.

'Car!' she said, pointing out into the road.

'Yes, there are lots of cars aren't there?' I grinned. 'Can you see Nana's car?'

As soon as the words left my mouth, my eyes rested on

one car in particular. Parked across the road from mine was a familiar car.

A small red one with a gaffer-taped wing mirror.

'No way,' I gasped. 'This is just too much.'

Anger bubbled up inside me as I marched across the living room and out of the front door of Louisa's flat.

'Are you OK, Maggie?' she shouted as I ran down the stairs.

'I'll be back in a minute,' I yelled. 'I just need to have a word with someone.'

This was once too often to be a coincidence. I stormed outside and marched towards Lee's car. I could see that he was sat in the front seat, his baseball cap pulled down over his face.

My heart was thumping as he looked up at me and suddenly I worried that I'd made the wrong decision. What had he come here for? What was I going to face? Maybe I'd just made the biggest mistake of my life.

EIGHT

Meetings and Meltdowns

Lee stared at me as I knocked furiously on the car window.

'What are you doing here?' I said through the glass. 'You can't keep following me like this. 'I'm at a friend's house and this isn't acceptable.'

I didn't want him to know exactly whose house it was or to think this was where I lived as I didn't want to put Louisa and her family at risk.

'Please wind down the window so I can talk to you,' I asked.

I was trying to appear calm but inside, my heart was racing.

Lee showed no reaction. He now just stared straight ahead, a blank look in his eyes.

'I'm going to have to call Patsy and tell her about his,' I told him. 'If you're trying to scare me then it's not working.'

Eventually he leant over and wound down the window. I took a deep breath and prepared myself for a barrage of abuse.

'I-I'm sorry,' he said quietly. 'I ain't trying to scare you or cause no trouble.'

I looked at him, confused. I'd expected to be met with threats and aggression but his voice was shaking with what sounded like nerves.

'Lee, what are you doing here?' I asked him. 'Have you been following me?'

He looked down and nodded.

'Why? I said. 'It's not an appropriate thing for you to do.'

'I-I-I just wanted to give you some clothes for Bobby,' he said in a quiet voice. 'I know Brianna gave you some for the girls but Bobby didn't get none. Well, nothing decent anyway. I want him to have proper stuff, nice things, like them.'

He gestured to the passenger seat where there were a couple of carrier bags.

'Lee, this isn't the right way to go about this,' I told him. 'If you and Brianna had clothes for Bobby then you should have brought them to one of the contact sessions and Palvi would have passed them on to me. Just like she did with the things for the girls.'

'I couldn't,' he said, still not making eye contact with me. 'I didn't want Bri to know.'

This was getting more confusing by the minute.

'Why, Lee?' I asked. 'Why wouldn't you want Brianna to know?'

He shrugged.

'I just didn't,' he mumbled.

I didn't want to ask him any more questions or engage him in more conversation. I needed to get him away from here in case he suddenly turned nasty or aggressive.

'Just this once, I'll make an exception and take the clothes for Bobby,' I told him. 'But I want you to leave now and please don't follow me ever again. I will have to tell Patsy about this and if it happens again, she'll have no choice but to get the police involved.'

Lee looked up at me with panic in his eyes.

'OK, I'm going,' he mumbled. 'But please don't tell Brianna I've given them to you.'

'I can't promise that I'm afraid,' I said. 'That's up to Patsy.'

He leant over and opened the passenger door and gestured for me to take the two carrier bags off the front seat.

'Thank you,' I said. 'I'll make sure Bobby gets them.'

He nodded.

'Can I ask you one more question?' he mumbled and I nodded.

'How's Bobby doing?'

'He's OK,' I said. 'But if you want to know any more about Bobby then you've got to go through Patsy or talk to him yourself.

'Really, I shouldn't even be speaking to you now, but I'll let Patsy know that I've taken the clothes and that we've had this conversation.'

He nodded.

As I shut the passenger door, he turned his keys in the ignition. I stood on the pavement and watched as the red car disappeared off down Louisa's road.

When I walked back, Louisa was waiting in the entrance hall to the flats holding Edie in her arms.

'Is everything OK, Maggie?' she asked, concerned. 'I didn't know whether to come out or not.'

'No, you did the right thing, lovey,' I told her. 'It was just somebody who wanted a word with me.'

I didn't want to worry her by telling her what had happened. To be honest, Lee hadn't been aggressive in any way but I was still unnerved by the whole experience. It was creepy thinking someone had been following me and there was something decidedly odd about him and the way he wouldn't make eye contact with me most of the time.

'Are you sure you're OK?' Louisa asked again. 'You look a little bit shaken up.'

'Honestly, I'm absolutely fine,' I told her.

I stayed for another half an hour but my mind was racing thinking about what had just happened. As soon as I left Louisa's flat, I nervously scanned the road looking for the red car. On the ten-minute drive home, I was constantly looking in my rear-view mirror to make sure that Lee wasn't following me back to my house. When I was convinced the coast was clear, I hurried up the front path and closed the door safely behind me. Only then did I breathe a sigh of relief and feel my shoulders relax. Even though Lee hadn't been threatening, his behaviour had really unnerved me.

I got my phone out of my bag and called Patsy to let her know what had happened.

'Gosh, I'm sorry, Maggie, that must have been really scary for you,' she said.

'It was just all a bit odd,' I told her. 'He wasn't aggressive or abusive but it's weird that he followed me just to give me some clothes for Bobby. And why all the secrecy around not telling Brianna?'

As well as speaking to the parents together, Patsy said they were due to talk to them separately over the next few days.

'It's certainly something we can raise with Lee when we get him on his own,' she told me. 'It's all very strange and it must have been really unsettling for you.'

'It really was,' I nodded. 'Do you think it's worth contacting the police?'

'Sadly, I don't actually think there's anything they could do,' she told me.

I knew she was right. Unless there was a restraining order out on Lee, he had a right to be anywhere that he wanted. He hadn't turned up at my address and the children hadn't been with me at the time. From his point of view, he could argue that he was just sitting in his car on a random road, minding his own business when I'd approached him.

'Hopefully Lee has got the message now and it won't happen again,' Becky said when I called her to tell her what had happened.

'I really hope so,' I replied. 'I know I'm going to spend the next few days constantly looking over my shoulder.'

As soon as I put the phone down, I unpacked the carrier bags that Lee had given me. They were full of brand new clothes, all with their labels still on. Pairs of trousers, tops, a coat, pants, socks and shoes. Lee had obviously bought them all new for Bobby.

It was all very odd. I honestly didn't know what to think any more.

I took the tags off the clothes and hung them up in Bobby's wardrobe. I didn't say anything to him or the girls about them as I didn't want to make a big deal about where they had come from. Bobby had got so used to wearing new clothes at my house, I didn't think he'd ask about these new items.

*

That night while dinner was in the oven, I sat with Bobby at the kitchen table as he had some phonics to do. The girls were lying on the floor over the other side of the kitchen making some bracelets.

As we went through the sounds in his reading book, I could see Bobby was finding it hard to read some of the words.

'Take your time,' I told him gently. 'There's no rush. There are some really tricky sounds here.'

I could see that he was trying so hard but he was really struggling. Two pages in, he suddenly stopped, shut the book and burst into tears.

'Hey, what is it?' I soothed, putting my arm around him.

They were deep, juddering sobs that made his frail little body shake.

'I can't do it,' he wailed. 'I'm thick and I'm useless.'

'Bobby,' I gasped. 'That's not true.'

'It is,' he said angrily, pulling away from me. 'I'm a stupid idiot.'

Then, much to my horror, he started hitting himself.

'Stupid, stupid, stupid,' he chanted as he whacked himself on the head again and again.

Gently but firmly, I grabbed his hands and slowly moved them away from his face. Then I pulled him into a hug.

'Bobby,' I said, trying to get through to him. 'You're not useless and you're certainly not stupid and don't let anyone ever tell you that.'

As I cuddled him, I glanced over my shoulder to see Melodie and Poppy on the other side of the room. They were staring at

Bobby, but what disturbed me most was the look on Melodie's face. She was smirking.

'Come on,' I told Bobby, ignoring her. 'Let's put this book away and we'll try it again another time.'

Ten minutes later, dinner was ready so I got the girls and Bobby sitting at the table while I dished up.

'Nearly there,' I told them as I bent down to take the lasagne out of the oven. 'The garlic bread needs five more minutes.'

As I was getting out the plates, out of the corner of my eye I could see Melodie whispering something into Bobby's ear. Bobby was frozen like a statue, a terrified look on his face.

As I walked back to the table, I caught the tale end of it.

'. . . and you're a stupid idiot who can't read,' she whispered.

'Melodie!' I said. 'I heard exactly what you just said to Bobby. I don't want nasty and mean people at my table so get down please.'

'But . . .' she stuttered, looking horrified. 'I was only telling the truth.'

'You were being mean and hurtful,' I told her. 'Now get down please and go into the living room.'

Poppy and Bobby both sat there in silence.

'Are you OK, flower?' I asked him. 'That wasn't a very nice thing for Melodie to say and besides, it's completely untrue.'

He nodded meekly but I wasn't sure that he believed me.

I went into the living room where Melodie was sitting sulkily on the sofa.

'Can I have my dinner now?' she asked.

'You can but I want you to apologise to your brother for being so rude and mean to him.'

'He's not my brother,' she replied.

'Melodie,' I said. 'I will not tolerate that sort of behaviour in this house so go and say sorry to Bobby.'

'But why?' she moaned.

'Because you can't treat people like that,' I told her.

Melodie didn't seem bothered at all; the only thing she was shocked and sorry about was that someone had pulled her up on her behaviour. She was so sneaky about it; if she didn't think an adult was listening, she was all too happy to be vile to him.

After dinner, I put the TV on for the children in the living room while I cleared up in the kitchen. Ten minutes later, I went to go and check on them and see if they wanted a drink. As I walked down the hallway, I heard them talking. Something made me stop and linger in the doorway for a few seconds.

'I don't care what she says, you are an idiot,' said Melodie.

'You are a stupid pants, you are a stupid pants,' chanted Poppy in a sing-song voice.

'You're right, Poppy,' added Melodie. 'He's soooo stupid.'

I peered through the crack in the doorframe. Bobby was sat in the chair with his head lowered, with Melodie stood over him.

'Look at me,' she hissed. 'Did you hear what I said, stupid?'

She crouched down next to him and raised her hand in the air as if she was about to hit him. Bobby flinched and covered his face with his hands for protection.

'Melodie!' I shouted, bursting through the door.

She looked shocked and jumped away.

'I ain't touched him,' she said quickly.

Bobby was cowering in fear on the chair.

'Come with me right now,' I told her firmly.

I marched her to the kitchen.

'Put your bottom on that chair and don't move,' I said. 'I'm going to check on your brother and make sure that he's OK.'

'I told you, he ain't my brother,' she said sulkily.

'I don't want to hear another word from you unless it's an apology to Bobby.'

Melodie glared at me.

I went back to the living room where Poppy and Bobby were sat in silence.

I crouched down by Bobby and gave him a hug.

'Are you OK?' I asked him and he nodded meekly.

'Come on, flower, you come with me, let's go and get you a drink. Don't worry, I won't let anybody hurt you.'

We went into the kitchen along with Poppy. Melodie was still sitting on the chair.

Bobby stared at the floor and pressed himself into my leg.

'Melodie, what do you say to Bobby?' I asked her. 'We do not hit people in this house and I will not tolerate behaviour like that.'

She sat there with her hands folded defiantly across her chest.

'Melodie,' I said again.

'OK,' she sighed. 'Sorry.'

It was a close shave and I had got there in the nick of time before things were about to get physical. I knew from now on, I couldn't risk leaving Melodie in the same room as Bobby. I needed to keep him safe so, wherever I was in the house, I had to bring Melodie with me. She hated every minute of it but I was determined to teach her a lesson and make her realise that she couldn't treat Bobby like that.

*

The children had been with me for just over two weeks when it was time for a Looked After Child (LAC) review. It was normally held at Social Services and key figures involved in the children's lives would attend to help decide what was going to happen to them going forwards.

Attending LAC reviews were an essential part of a foster carer's role and I was looking forward to this one to see if we could find out any more about Melodie, Poppy and Bobby and their home life.

It was being chaired by the children's Independent Reviewing Officer, or IRO. An IRO was someone who worked for Social Services but who wasn't directly involved in the case. They are there to advocate for the children and to make sure the right processes are being followed. Melodie, Poppy and Bobby's IRO was a man called Colin. He was an ex-social worker and, we'd worked together several times over the years. He was a really compassionate, funny man who was brilliant with children.

'Maggie!' he grinned as I walked into the meeting room.

'It's so lovely to see you, Colin,' I said, giving him a hug.

It had been a few years since we'd last seen each other as he'd moved on from social work and he was a full-time IRO these days.

I wasn't sure if Brianna and Lee would be there but there was no sign of them around the table as I sat down.

'No Mum and Dad?' I asked Patsy.

'They were invited but they declined to come,' she shrugged.

There were quite a few of us squeezed into the small meeting room. As well as Patsy and Becky, there was also

Palvi, the contact worker. There was also a stern-looking, grey-haired woman who I didn't recognise.

'This is Anne Nichols, the deputy head at the school,' said Patsy introducing her.

'DC Orton sends her apologies that no one from the police is available to attend today,' said Colin, starting off the meeting.

He turned to Anne first as she needed to get back to school.

'What are your impressions of the children?' Colin asked her.

'On the face of it, it's like they're from two different families,' she told everyone. 'Bobby has been on our radar for a while and his teacher has had a number of concerns.'

She described how the girls had joined the school just over three years ago, after they'd moved to the area. Bobby had started a year later.

'We've never had any issues with the girls,' Mrs Nichols told us. 'They've always been clean, well presented, have all their equipment and dinner money. They're confident in class, there are no behavioural concerns and they're doing OK academically.'

'Bobby is the complete opposite.'

She described how his uniform was often so dirty and worn, they had to give him clothes to wear from lost property. He never had a PE kit or a coat and his dinner money mostly went unpaid.

'According to their class teachers, Mum attends all of the parents' evenings, assemblies and concerts for the girls,' she said. 'No one has ever been to any of Bobby's.'

'What about Dad?' asked Colin.

'No one has ever seen Dad to the point that we thought Brianna was a single mother,' she sighed.

Brianna was listed as the only contact for all three children.

'Bobby's teacher, both last year's and this one, has called Mum several times but she's never got back to them.'

Mrs Nichols described how they'd had ongoing concerns about Bobby being very withdrawn in class. He didn't engage or make friends easily and would often wet himself.

'Obviously when we saw the bruises, it immediately became a safeguarding issue and we had to get Social Services involved.'

Even though no one from the police was in attendance, Colin read out an update from DC Orton.

'Liz Orton sent an email confirming that both parents have been interviewed, both refused to answer any questions and, at this stage, there are no charges to answer to, although the case remains open.'

Then it was Palvi's turn to address the meeting. She talked about contact and how the parents had been.

'Brianna and the girls have a strong bond,' she said. 'They're clearly very close.'

'And what about Lee?' asked Colin.

'It's very odd as the girls have very little to do with him,' added Palvi. 'In a way it's like he's not there; they barely acknowledge him. Even he and Bobby hardly say anything to each other.'

'Do you think the children are scared of him?' said Colin.

'It could be that,' replied Patsy. 'Lee regularly turns up at contact with black eyes or bruises and Brianna has talked about how he gets into fights at the pub. Although none of the kids themselves have ever said anything explicitly about that.'

Patsy told the meeting that I believed that Lee had been following me.

'Gosh, I'm sorry to hear that, Maggie,' said Colin. 'That must have been really unsettling for you. Was he threatening towards you?'

'No, not at all,' I said. 'His behaviour wasn't aggressive or anything, it was just strange.'

I described how he'd given me the clothes for Bobby but hadn't wanted Brianna to know.

'What are your observations of the children, Maggie?' Colin asked finally.

I talked about the girls' behaviour towards Bobby.

'To be honest, it's mainly Melodie but sometimes Poppy joins in too,' I said. 'She thinks they can get away with being aggressive, nasty and violent to Bobby whenever she wants. Whenever they're around, he's very quiet and withdrawn and I would go as far to say he's even fearful of them.

'They've clearly learnt this behaviour from somewhere and I can only guess that it's something that they're used to from home.'

Colin looked up from his notes.

'Have you witnessed the girls being violent to Bobby?'

'The other day I stepped in when Melodie was about to hit him,' I told them.

'Do we think Bobby's injuries could have been caused by the girls?'

Patsy shook her head.

'Both the police and the GP looked at Bobby's bruises at the time and thought they were finger marks from adult-sized hands.'

'I agree that it's as if the children are from two different households,' I said. 'If we go out, the girls ask for things from the shop. They expect food and drinks to be bought for them and anything else that they fancy. They complain about the meals I make and the clothes I give them. Nothing is ever good enough.

'With Bobby, there is no expectation there whatsoever. He seems eternally grateful that there's regular food on the table and clothes to wear and never asks for anything.

'I also get the feeling that his overriding sense is that he doesn't deserve anything, that he's stupid and not good enough. Sadly that's how the girls treat him too.'

'We obviously need to get to the bottom of where that has come from,' nodded Colin.

'Our main issue here is that no one is saying anything,' sighed Patsy. 'Both parents are still maintaining they know nothing about Bobby's injuries and how he got them.'

I could see that Colin's brow was furrowed in concentration as he made notes.

'It's all very confusing and it's hard to get a full picture if the parents aren't cooperating with us,' he agreed. 'We clearly can't let the children return home while there are all these unanswered questions. I think we need more time to do a bit more digging.'

Colin said that he thought a six-week parenting assessment of both parents was the best way forward.

'That way we can try to ascertain what was going on in that house with Bobby and if the children are safe,' he said.

I agreed with his decision. An assessment would involve sessions with Brianna and Lee together and separately, where social workers would delve into their relationship as well their beliefs about how children should be brought up. It would also look at their own childhoods and how that affected them as parents.

Whatever happened, all we could hope was that it would finally provided the answers that we were looking for.

NINE

Special Requests

The kitchen floor wasn't the comfiest place to sit and everywhere was covered in LEGO but I didn't mind. I could tell from the way that Bobby was quietly humming to himself as he played that he was really enjoying this.

'Look Maggie!' he said, tapping me on the arm. 'I made a spaceship.'

'That's amazing,' I smiled as I looked at his creation. 'Much better than the boring old car that I built.'

'But that's good too,' he said sweetly.

I'd enrolled the girls in a weekly dance class at a local church hall. Despite Melodie and Poppy's protest on the first week, I thought they were enjoying it. It was an hour-and-a-half class and by the time we walked there and back, it gave Bobby and I an hour at home together.

I was really keen for him to have this one-to-one time with me. Without the girls around, he really seemed to come out of his shell. He'd got the confidence both to play freely and to talk to me.

I loved hearing him chatter away and I was starting to see what a sweet, good-natured little lad he was.

'I like being at your house, Maggie,' he told me as he started to build another creation.

'Well, I am very pleased about that,' I smiled. 'What do you like about it?'

'I like all the toys and playing in the garden,' he said.

'Do you have a garden at your house?' I asked him and he shook his head.

'I like playing on the bike and the scooter,' he continued, as he clicked the bricks together. 'And the LEGO and the big box of cars that you have. And I like your house because I'm always good so I can have food.'

'Can't you always have food at your house?' I asked him, reaching for some more bricks.

'No,' he said.

'And I like my bedroom at your house,' he said, quickly changing the subject.

'What do you like about it?' I asked him.

'I don't have no one else there,' he said. 'And I like the books and the little light and the soft and fluffy bed.'

'Is your bed at home soft and fluffy too?' I asked him and he shook his head.

'I don't have no bed at home, silly,' he smiled. 'I sleep here.'

He tapped the floor next to him.

I did my best not to show any reaction, as I didn't want him to think that I was judging him.

'But the floor's very hard,' I said. 'Surely that can't be very comfy for you?'

'Yes, but I've got a special trick,' he smiled. 'I get the cushions from the sofa and put them in a row and make a special bed.'

'Is that just sometimes?' I asked him. 'I bet you do have a soft and fluffy bed other times?'

'No,' he said, shaking his head. 'All the time.'

My heart ached to hear how matter-of-fact he was about having to sleep on cushions on the floor.

'What about Melodie and Poppy?' I asked. 'Do they sleep on the floor too?'

He shook his head.

'No, they've got beds like you've got,' he told me. 'They're not naughty so they're allowed to have them.'

'Are you naughty, Bobby?' I asked him and he nodded.

'What do you do that's naughty?' I asked him and he shrugged.

Then he looked down at the floor.

'I'm very, very bad,' he said quietly. 'I don't deserve to have nice things. Nobody loves me.'

I was heartbroken to hear this little boy say those words and to think so little of himself.

'Who says that to you, Bobby?' I asked him gently. 'Who tells you that you're bad?'

Bobby didn't answer and started adding more bricks to his creation. It was as if someone had flicked a switch and he had suddenly clammed up again.

'Look, I made a rocket,' he said, holding up his LEGO and avoiding answering my question.

'This is a good rocket,' he said. 'I bet it goes really fast when it shoots into space.'

Bobby lay on the floor pretending to launch the rocket and I knew our conversation was over. I didn't press him any more and let him play. I knew that if I asked him another direct question, he was likely to go quiet again and I didn't want that. It was better to leave things open-ended and wait for him to share things in his own time.

Fifteen minutes later, as we walked down the road to go and collect the girls, I felt his little hand reach for mine.

'Can we do LEGO again, Maggie?' he asked.

'Yes, lovey,' I said, giving Bobby's hand a little squeeze. 'Of course we can.'

All I could hope was that little by little, he would open up and we would finally get to the bottom of who had been treating him so badly.

That evening I wrote up all of my notes from the day so I could email them to Becky and Patsy. As I typed out the conversation that Bobby and I had had earlier, I felt even sadder.

Not being 'allowed' food and not having a bed to sleep in was shocking, but it was the words that he had used to describe himself that had really got to me.

I'm bad. Nobody loves me.

Who would be so cruel as to make an eight-year-old feel like that?

Patsy rang me the following morning for a catch-up and we talked about what Bobby had said.

'It's good that he's starting to open up to you,' she told me. 'We need him to carry on talking to find out what was really going on at home.'

I was keen to know how contact had been going.

Although I took the children to the contact centre twice a week, I didn't sit in on the sessions and waited outside. As foster carers we don't usually become involved in contact. We might drop off and pick up, but we avoid going into sessions as much as possible. We're the child's safe space so it's important to separate ourselves from birth parents.

As the LAC review had decided on a parenting assessment, Patsy had attended the last couple of sessions to see for herself how the children were interacting with Lee and Brianna.

'Not an awful lot seems to have changed,' she said. 'Brianna and the girls tend to chat but Bobby and his dad just sit there. Palvi's tried her best but as you know, that's not her role.'

A contact worker's job was to supervise a session and record what happened. It wasn't her responsibility to entertain them.

'Palvi said she'd put some toys out at the start of the session but Bobby hadn't shown any interest in them and Lee hadn't tried to get him involved,' Patsy told me.

'At the session I went to she'd even set up a game for them,' she added. 'But it just seemed really forced and stilted between Bobby and his dad. They played it but there was no fun or laughter or even chatter between them. Bobby wouldn't even make eye contact with Lee.'

'What was Lee like with Bobby?' I asked.

'Exactly the same. He didn't make any effort to really talk or engage with his son.'

Patsy described how it hadn't been any better between Brianna and Bobby – there was zero interaction between them.

'I think when we have the individual sessions, it will really give me a chance to talk to both her and Lee about their relationship with Bobby,' said Patsy.

She described how during one of the contact sessions that she had attended, Palvi had encouraged Brianna to join in with the game that Bobby and Lee were playing but she had refused.

'She said that there was no point as Bobby always spoils everything. She really hasn't got a nice word to say about him.'

The picture Brianna painted of Bobby as argumentative, difficult and destructive was totally at odds with the quiet, gentle little boy who was living at my house.

'It's not hard to see why the girls treat Bobby the way they do,' I sighed. 'It's obviously learnt behaviour from home.'

'I think there is definitely emotional abuse there,' said Patsy. 'As for the physical side of things, we still need to find out more.

'As we know, Dad has got a past history of aggression,' Patsy continued. 'Palvi says he's turned up at contact a few times with a black eye and we know that he followed you.'

'That was creepy and very unsettling but he was never aggressive,' I told her.

'How are the kids after contact?' Patsy asked me.

'The girls are always very tearful and clinging on to Mum, but Bobby can't get out of that room fast enough,' I told her.

In the car home, he always seemed to be feeling a mixture of relief and exhaustion.

'At least we know Mum's capable of emotion, I suppose,' I added.

'Yes, Brianna's very loving with the girls,' she replied.

'When Bobby's with me, he never talks about either parent,' I told Patsy. 'Whereas the girls are constantly asking about Mum and when they can go home.'

As everyone around the children had pointed out, it was like they were from two different homes.

'It's one of the most puzzling cases I've dealt with,' sighed Patsy.

'I struggle to see how Brianna and Lee ever got together,' I shrugged.

'Yep,' agreed Patsy.

Who knew what went on behind closed doors? Perhaps it was a relationship based on fear?

But fear of whom?

A few days later, there was another contact session. As usual, I picked the children up after school and took them. I did what I always did and sat in reception with a cup of tea while I tackled some paperwork.

I was just going through some bills when Louisa rang me.

'I can't hear you very well, lovey,' I told her. 'The reception's not great in here. I'll pop outside and ring you back.'

I put my coat on and went and sat on the wall at the front of the contact centre. Louisa was ringing for a catch-up so we had a ten-minute chat. I'd just hung up when the door to the contact centre swung open. My stomach sank when I saw who was walking towards me.

Lee.

He looked embarrassed to see me and avoided making eye contact. But I couldn't not say anything and ignore him.

'Hello Lee,' I said and he gave me a quick nod of acknowledgement.

I noticed a lighter in his hand so he'd obviously popped outside for a cigarette. I hadn't seen him since he'd followed me to Louisa's house as he'd always been in the contact room when I'd dropped the kids off. Being around him made me uncomfortable and I didn't want to make forced conversation with him.

I stood up.

'Best get back inside into the warm,' I said to him.

He nodded and as he took a drag on his cigarette, I noticed a deep laceration on his neck.

'Ouch, that looks nasty,' I said.

I hadn't intended to start a conversation but the words just slipped out.

'Oh er, yeah,' he said, pulling up the collar of his jacket self-consciously. 'The cat scratched me.'

'Cats can be really vicious,' I nodded. 'It looks very deep.'

As I turned to go back into the contact centre, Lee suddenly leant towards me and grabbed my arm. My heart started thumping; I wasn't sure what he was going to do.

'How's Bobby doing?' he asked in a quiet voice.

It was such a strange thing to say when he had spent the past half an hour with his son.

'Why don't you ask him yourself, Lee?' I suggested. 'That's what these sessions are for. To spend time with Bobby and chat to him.'

He looked down at the floor.

'I can't,' he said, shaking his head. 'Bobby won't talk to me.'

He paused.

'Why won't he talk to you, Lee?' I asked him.

He looked up at me and I noticed that his eyes were filled with tears.

'Cos he's scared of me,' he replied. 'I can see it in his eyes.'

I knew that it wasn't really my place to do this but I had to ask him the question.

'Why is Bobby scared of you. Lee?'

As the words left my mouth, I held my breath. Perhaps finally we were going to get some answers.

I was surprised to see that Lee was crying.

'It's all my fault,' he wept. 'I've let him down – he hates me.'

'How have you let him down?' I asked. 'Please tell me, Lee.'

Suddenly the door to the contact centre swung open. It was Brianna.

'Lee!' she said. 'That ciggy's taking forever and Palvi was wondering where you were.'

'Sorry,' he mumbled, quickly wiping his eyes.

I gave a nod of acknowledgement to Brianna but she ignored me and the pair of them walked back into the contact centre together.

I sighed and sat back down on the wall. What the heck had just happened there? It felt like Lee was about to reveal something significant.

There was still half an hour of the session left so I decided to call Patsy right then and tell her what had happened. I was paranoid of anyone hearing me so I went and sat in my car.

I described exactly what Lee had said to me.

'Do you think he was about to confess to something?' she asked.

'Who knows?' I told her. 'But he definitely said Bobby hated him and was scared of him.'

'That would make sense if he was the one who'd hurt him,' said Patsy. 'I think I need to talk to Lee separately as soon as possible.'

It was a normal part of a parenting assessment to do sessions with parents separately as well as together. Perhaps this was the way that we would all finally get some answers?

A couple of days later I was doing some cleaning while the kids were at school when I saw Patsy's number pop up on my mobile.

'How are things?' I said.

'Maggie, I've actually got a favour to ask you,' she said. 'I had a session with Lee today.'

'Oh good,' I replied. 'How did it go?'

'Not great,' she sighed. 'It was a struggle to get anything much out of him.'

My heart sank. She described how he was very guarded, particularly when it came to Bobby.

'I said for Bobby's sake, he had to tell us more,' she continued. 'And he got quite upset at one point but then he clammed up again. He kept saying the same thing.'

'What was that?' I asked.

'He said he would only talk if you were there.'

'Me?' I said, surprised. 'But Lee hardly knows me.'

'He said that you were the only one he trusts because he can see that Bobby is happy with you,' she told me.

'So I wondered . . .' she said. 'I know it's not normally the done thing, but I thought I would ask you first to see how you felt about it. Would you consider sitting in on Lee's next session?'

'I'd lead it, of course, and ask all of the questions,' she reassured me. 'Your role would be to just be there and listen in the hope that he starts opening up.'

In my entire fostering career, I'd never been directly involved in any meetings like this. It was highly unusual for a foster carer to have anything to do with a parenting assessment.

It was a bit of an odd request as I wasn't close to Lee. Outside the centre the other night was the most I'd ever spoken to him.

'It worries me a bit to be honest,' I said.

'I know it's an unusual request, Maggie, but I'm willing to try anything that will allow Lee to open up,' begged Patsy.

'I can assure you I will do all the talking and ask the questions,' she replied. 'I think Lee just wants you there for reassurance.'

To be honest, the entire thing made me nervous. Why had Lee asked for me to be there? Was it some sort of power game for his own ego or entertainment? I knew there was only one way to find out.

'OK,' I agreed. 'I'll do it.'

TEN

Secrets and Lies

Nerves swirled in my stomach as I pushed open the door of the room at the contact centre. I was here to sit in on the session with Patsy and Lee in the hope that it would help him to start talking.

I still felt uneasy about being at this meeting but Lee had asked and I was prepared to do it for Bobby's sake. In all of this, he was my number one priority.

When I went in, Patsy and Lee were already sat there.

'Morning, Maggie,' smiled Patsy. 'I'll let you get your coat off then I'll make us all a cup of tea.'

'Hello Lee,' I said, looking over at him.

'Hi,' he said quietly, shifting his feet around.

We were in one of the smaller rooms at the contact centre that were usually used for counselling sessions or meetings with parents. It was slightly warmer and less damp than the main rooms thanks to the fan heater in the corner, but it was still run-down. There were two worn armchairs and a shabby sofa with a chipped wooden coffee table in the middle.

Lee and Patsy were sitting on the chairs so I plonked myself down on the sofa.

Patsy went over to the table in the corner of the room and flicked the white plastic kettle on.

'Lee, following our conversation the other day, Maggie has agreed to sit in on our chat,' she told him as she popped a tea bag in three polystyrene cups.

'Thanks,' he nodded, still avoiding making eye contact with me.

'That's OK,' I told him. 'If it helps Bobby then I'm willing to be here.'

Patsy handed us both a cup of tea then sat back down. She got a notebook and a pen out of her bag and turned to Lee, who took a swig of his tea before putting it down.

'So, Lee,' she began. 'The other day we started to talk about Bobby and I thought it would be good for us to have a bit of background about your family. Can you tell us about Bobby's biological mum?'

'Caz,' he shrugged. 'She turned out to be a druggy. He was only a baby when she went off the rails. She couldn't get off it, sold all our stuff.'

'Does Bobby ever see her?'

He shook his head.

'We ain't seen or heard nothing from her since he was nine months old. Me and my mam brought him up on our own.'

Lee described how since his mum had died four years ago, it had just been him and Bobby.

'That must have been hard for you, being a single dad,' Patsy nodded.

He shrugged.

'We got by,' he replied. 'He's a good kid.'

This was the first opportunity I'd had to really sit and observe Lee. In fact, it was the most that I'd ever heard him speak as when Brianna was around, he hardly said a word. As I watched him talk, I suddenly realised who he reminded me of. It was the way he stared at the floor and wouldn't make eye contact. It was his clothes too. Everything was worn and shabby, from his frayed jeans that looked way too big for him, to his sweatshirt that had holes in it and his trainers that were coming apart at the toes.

It was Bobby.

I started to think that perhaps I'd misjudged him. Was what I'd thought of as creepy or weird actually shyness, or a lack of confidence?

Then Patsy started to talk to him about Brianna and how they'd first met.

Lee stared at the floor.

'How long have you two been together?' Patsy asked him.

'Dunno,' he said. 'Two years.'

He described how they'd met in a local pub that he used to go to when a neighbour babysat for him. They'd quickly moved in together a couple of months later.

'What was it that attracted you to her?' Patsy asked.

Lee shrugged.

'There must have been something that made you two get together?'

'Suppose I was lonely,' he sighed. 'I was skint and fed up of struggling on my own. Bri was divorced and had a two-bed council flat that was bigger than mine.'

'So you and Bobby moved in with her?' asked Patsy, and he nodded.

Lee reached for his tea and as he did, I noticed that his hand was shaking. I also spotted three or four small red marks on his wrist that looked like burns.

'How did Brianna get on with Bobby?' Patsy asked him.

He shifted uncomfortably in his seat.

'Can I go for a slash?' he asked, quickly changing the subject.

'Yes, of course,' Patsy told him. 'The toilet's just outside on the right.'

As soon as he left the room, Patsy and I turned to each other.

'That's the most he's ever said,' she told me. 'I've spoken to him and Brianna several times and he's hardly said a word.'

'I was thinking exactly the same,' I agreed. 'I'm starting to think I got the wrong end of the stick about him. Listening to him talk and seeing his mannerisms – I think I found him weird and creepy, but I think perhaps he's just shy and lacking in confidence. Just like Bobby is.'

'You could be right,' sighed Patsy. 'He's certainly very nervy and on edge.'

I was about to say that he had looked uncomfortable talking about Brianna, when the door opened. Lee came back in, wiping his hands on his jeans.

'Where were we?' asked Patsy when he'd sat back down again. 'Oh yes, we were chatting about you and Brianna moving in together. How did you get on with Brianna's daughters Melodie and Poppy?'

'Bri spoils them and I didn't think they were ever gonna like me cos they didn't like sharing their mam with no one else.'

'And how did the girls get on with Bobby?' asked Patsy.

Lee paused.

'Not that good,' he said, scratching his nose.

Up until now it had all been fairly easy questions, but Patsy swiftly moved on.

'So, as you know, Lee, Bobby's teacher noticed some bruises on his arms,' she said. 'There were also some older, faded bruises on his back too . . .'

'Can you tell us how he got those bruises, Lee?'

He looked away and shook his head.

'Dunno,' he said.

'The doctor who examined Bobby at the time felt the bruises on his arms had been caused by someone grabbing Bobby with significant force,' continued Patsy. 'She also felt they were caused by adult-sized hands rather than something that might have happened when Bobby was playing with other children. Do you know which adult might have hurt Bobby?'

Lee picked at the skin around one of his fingernails and shook his head again.

Undeterred, Patsy carried on with her questions.

'Over the past few weeks, Bobby has opened up to Maggie and told her things about his life at home with you and Brianna,' she said.

Lee looked up at me.

'What's he been telling you?' he asked, his face etched with worry.

I didn't know what to say to him and I was all too aware that I was supposed to be there as an observer. But Patsy thankfully jumped in.

'Bobby told Maggie about the fact that he regularly went without food, he didn't have a bed to sleep on and he wasn't allowed any clothes or nice things.'

Lee's face crumpled and he turned to me.

'What else did he say?' he asked me.

Although it felt deeply uncomfortable, I knew I had to answer him honestly and truthfully.

'He said that he didn't deserve any of those things because he was bad and that nobody loved him.'

Lee buried his head in his hands.

'Lee, I know this must be hard for you to hear but what can you tell us about this?' Patsy asked him. 'Why was Bobby treated this way while Melodie and Poppy seemed to be clean and comfortable?

'We've spoken to Bobby's teachers and they told us how he never had a clean uniform, that nobody came to his parents' evenings or paid his dinner money. Everyone that we have talked to is telling us that this is a child who wasn't being cared for or loved.'

Lee suddenly let out a whimper.

'He is loved!' he wept. 'I love him. I swear I do. I've let him down.'

His whole body shook as he sobbed into his hands.

'How have you let Bobby down, Lee?' Patsy asked.

I held my breath, waiting for his answer.

'He's scared of me,' Lee cried. 'I can see it in his eyes. I can't live with the guilt. It's all my fault.'

'What do you feel guilty about?' Patsy asked him gently. She paused.

'Lee, did you hurt Bobby? Life is stressful and we understand that sometimes, when things get too much, people can lose their temper . . .'

Lee shook his head.

'No no!' he cried. 'I swear I ain't never laid a finger on him. I'd never hurt my lad.'

He looked up at us.

'I ain't done nothing. But that's the problem.'

He buried his head in his hands again.

'Lee, if you didn't hurt Bobby then can you tell us who did?' urged Patsy. 'Our job is to protect Bobby and, if you love your son like you say you do, then you'll want to protect him too.'

He shook his head.

'It was her . . . It was Bri.'

Patsy and I looked at each other.

'So just to clarify, Lee, you're saying that it was Brianna who hurt Bobby and who caused those bruises on his arms?'

Lee nodded.

'She ain't never liked him. She hit him and she kicked him and sometimes she punched him. She treated him like s**t and made his life a misery. She told him that he was useless and a waste of space and she got her girls to say the same. The worst thing is, the poor lad started to believe it.'

He looked like a broken man as he stared up at us with bloodshot eyes.

It was horrific to hear and to think that any adult could do that to a little boy, especially a woman who had children of her own. Somehow it made it all the more shocking.

'Lee, why do you think Brianna acted that way towards Bobby?' Patsy asked. 'Did you ever try and stop her? Did you tell anybody else about what was happening at home?'

Suddenly Lee stood up.

'I can't do this no more,' he muttered, wiping away his tears. 'I'm going for a ciggy.'

As he walked out, Patsy and I looked at each other.

'Wow, I didn't expect that,' she sighed. 'Do you think he's telling the truth about Brianna?'

'He seemed genuine,' I replied. 'And as we know from experience, women hurt children too.'

'I'd better go outside and check that he's OK,' Patsy told me.

When she left the room, I took a sip of my tea but it was stone cold by then.

My instinct was that Lee was telling the truth but, whatever had happened, it was such a desperately sad situation. I had so many other questions whizzing around in my head.

If Brianna had hurt Bobby, why hadn't Lee done anything about it? Why hadn't he ended their relationship and left her, or told the police? Why hadn't he said anything up until now and exonerated himself?

A few minutes later, Lee and Patsy came back in the room. Lee had stopped crying but he looked like a broken man.

'What happens now?' he asked. 'Will I get into trouble?'

'To be honest with you, I don't know,' Patsy told him. 'I'll need to speak to my manager. I suspect what will happen first is that you will need to give a statement to the police telling them what you've just told us. Then I'm assuming they will bring Brianna in to be questioned again.'

Lee looked horrified.

'No, no way,' he said, his voice filled with panic. 'Please don't tell the police. Brianna will know that I've grassed her up.'

'Lee, if she's hurt Bobby, then she needs to face the consequences,' Patsy told him. 'She's broken the law. If she has hurt Bobby then why wouldn't you want her to be found out and punished?'

Lee shook his head.

'I was just messing with you,' he told us. 'What I said wasn't true. I was just making it up. Can't you just forget it?'

'Lee, I have to act on what you've told me,' Patsy explained. 'I can't ignore it – I have a duty to pass on that information.'

'Well I'll just deny it then,' he said matter-of-factly. 'I'll say that you're lying.'

I just couldn't understand it. Why would he want to protect someone who had hurt his son?

'Is it because you're worried that you'll get into trouble with the police too?' asked Patsy. 'I can't give you a 100 per cent guarantee, but it's likely they'll look on your situation with leniency as you're doing the right thing now.'

'I told you, I don't want the police involved,' he said. 'Please, I'm begging you.'

'Lee, we have to protect Bobby,' Patsy told him firmly.

'I'm begging you, please don't say anything,' he urged her.

Lee looked like he was about to burst into tears again.

'I can't do this,' he muttered. 'I'm sorry, I can't be here any more.'

He picked up his coat, got up and walked out.

Patsy immediately went after him while I sat in the meeting room and waited. Five minutes later she came back in.

'He's gone,' she shrugged. 'He said he didn't want to talk any more and he refused point-blank to come back in. He drove off.

'What a mess,' sighed Patsy. 'I know it will be hard for him but I don't understand his reluctance to get the police involved. Do you think he was making it up about Brianna hurting Bobby?' Patsy asked me.

'I think he was telling the truth,' I said. 'I could see how upset he was. Besides, why would he make something up like that?'

'But why didn't he do something then if she was hurting him?' asked Patsy. 'Why didn't he take Bobby and get out of there?'

'Sometimes it's easier to stay, I suppose.'

I knew there were all sorts of reasons people stayed in toxic relationships – money, the fear of being alone, some warped version of love.

The other question was, why had he gone back on what he'd said?

'I think he got scared,' said Patsy. 'I think he told us the truth and suddenly got frightened when he realised the implications.'

Parents had faced criminal charges in the past for knowing their partner was hurting their child and failing to prevent it or report it to anyone.

'I'll go and have a word with my manager now and explain what's happened,' Patsy told me. 'I'll give you a ring later, Maggie, and let you know what the plan is.'

'OK,' I said.

As I drove home, my head ached. I was convinced that Lee had been genuine and was telling us the truth this morning. But now we needed him to cooperate with both Social Services and the police. When was it all going to end?

When I got home, I called Becky to update her on how the meeting had gone.

'Lee said it was his partner who had been hurting Bobby,' I told her.

'Gosh, that's sad,' she said. 'But at least we're starting to get to the bottom of things.'

A couple of hours later, Patsy called.

'My manager agreed that we need to get the police involved. I called them and they're going to contact Lee now and tell him that he needs to come in and make another statement.'

'How did he react to that?' I asked her.

'I phoned to tell him what was going to happen but there was no answer so I left a voicemail.'

'But what if he refuses to give another statement or denies that it was Brianna who hurt Bobby?' I asked.

'We'll deal with that when we come to it,' said Patsy. 'Maybe when he talks to the police it will reassure him that perhaps he won't face prosecution or, if he does, they will take into account his mitigating circumstances.

'I'm glad you were there today, Maggie. At least there are two of us who heard him say what he did.'

'I'm happy to talk to the police if that helps,' I added.

'Thank you, I appreciate that,' she told me. 'But let's see what happens.'

The rest of the day passed in a blur. My head was still spinning from spending most of the morning sat in that small meeting room. So, when I picked the children up from school, I insisted on taking them to the park for half an hour in the hope that some fresh air would help clear my head.

The girls did nothing but moan.

'It's freezing,' said Melodie. 'I wanna go back.'

As I watched Bobby sitting on the swing on his own, I felt like crying.

This morning we'd got an idea of what this poor little lad had been put through at the hands of his dad's girlfriend. If I was confused about why Lee hadn't protected him, then what on earth must *he* be thinking?

Lee did seem to genuinely care about him though. All I could think about was the heartbreak on his face as I'd told him what Bobby had said to me about nobody loving him. To me, that had felt sincere. But at the same time, I was still confused. I never understood how someone could sit back and do nothing when they knew their partner was hurting their child. Why had Lee not left Brianna if she was treating Bobby so badly?

I hardly slept that night and it was still on my mind the following morning when I dropped the kids off at school. I headed straight back home and was just about to tackle a mountain of washing when there was a loud hammering on the front door.

'Coming!' I yelled.

More hammering. This time it was even louder and more urgent.

'Steady on!' I shouted. 'I said I'm coming.'

I opened the door to find a man stood on the doorstep. I didn't recognse him at first as he had a baseball cap pulled down low over his face.

'Can I help you?' I asked.

It was only when he looked up that I realised who it was.

'Lee!' I gasped. 'What the heck has happened to you?'

His face was literally black and blue. His lip was swollen and bleeding, he had gouges down the side of his face and a black eye that was so swollen he could barely open it.

'Please let me in,' he begged.

I could see he was struggling to talk as his mouth was full of blood.

Never in a million years would I normally have allowed a birth parent to come into my house who had turned up unannounced on my doorstep. But all procedure went out of the window when I saw the state Lee was in. Bobby and the girls were at school and I couldn't turn him away when he was this badly injured. There was no time for questions; he was shaking and I could tell that he was in shock.

'Thank you,' he said. 'I need you to help me, Maggie.'

ELEVEN

Home Truths

Adrenalin surged through me as Lee staggered through the door. I helped him through to the kitchen where I got him sat down.

His face was such a mess, I didn't know what to do first.

'Can I get you some water?' I asked and he nodded.

His hands were shaking as he picked up the glass and I saw him wince as he tried to take a sip with his bloody lip. His eye was so swollen it had almost closed.

'I'll get you some Ibuprofen and an ice pack,' I told him. 'That should help a bit with the pain.'

I could see Lee was in shock but I needed to ask him some questions.

'How did you know where I lived?' I asked him.

'Sorry,' he said, looking embarrassed. 'When I was trying to give you those clothes for Bobby, I followed you back from school one morning.

'But then I thought I best not turn up here, which is why I waited until another time, when you went to your friend's instead.

'I swear I didn't mean any harm,' he said. 'I would never hurt Bobby or put him in danger – I just wanted him to have some decent clothes.'

I nodded. It wasn't ideal but it was the least of my worries right now.

I knew in reality I should call Patsy and wait for her to get here before I asked him any questions but concern took over.

'Lee, what on earth happened?' I asked him. 'Who did this to you?'

Someone had really laid into him.

'Don't know,' he mumbled.

'Lee, now isn't the time to say silent. Someone has really hurt you.'

All sorts of scenarios were running through my mind. I knew he often came to contact with a black eye or a split lip after a brawl on a night out. Had he been involved in a fight at the pub last night or had someone attacked him on the way home?

'Have you been mugged?' I asked him. 'We really need to call the police. And I'm going to have to phone Patsy to let her know that you're here. And what about Brianna? Do you want me to ring her?'

'No,' gasped Lee. 'Please don't call her.'

'Were you attacked?' I asked him and he nodded.

'Do you know who did it?' I continued. 'Did you see their face?'

'I can't tell you,' he said meekly. 'I'm not saying nothing.'

I felt frustration bubbling up inside me. I could see that he was in a bad way but Lee needed to start telling us the truth otherwise no one could help him.

'Lee, you can't turn up on my doorstep in this kind of state and then refuse to tell me the truth about what's happened. We want to help you and make sure that you're OK. So please just tell me who did this to you. Do it for Bobby's sake, if nothing else.'

Lee stared down at the floor.

'It was Brianna,' he said quietly.

I thought I'd misheard him at first.

'Brianna?' I repeated, shocked. 'What do you mean?'

'Brianna did it,' he whispered. 'She attacked me.'

I could see the shame on Lee's face.

'But why?' I gasped.

'Patsy had left a voicemail on my phone saying the police wanted me to make another statement and she heard it because she had my phone and went off on one. She knew that I'd grassed her up about hurting Bobby.'

I was horrified, but one question quickly sprung into my mind.

'Has Brianna done this to you before?' I asked him.

He nodded.

'All the time,' he said.

Suddenly, everything that had happened over the past few weeks made sense. It explained the times Lee had turned up to contact with black eyes and split lips, and why he'd not told anyone about Brianna abusing Bobby.

'Why didn't you tell anyone that she was doing this to you?' I asked him.

'Cos I felt embarrassed,' he said quietly. 'What sort of bloke lets a woman beat the living crap out of him? I'm useless and pathetic.'

My heart went out to him. He sounded just like Bobby.

'None of this is your fault,' I told him. 'You're the victim here. Did you ever think about leaving her?'

'All the time,' he sighed. 'I wanted me and Bobby to get out of there but I was so scared . . . You don't know what she's like,' he continued. 'She told me that if I ever tried to leave then she'd kill Bobby, and I believed her. She took everything I had, so I didn't have no money,' he added. 'To buy those clothes for Bobby, I had to steal cash from her purse.'

'I'm so sorry that you've had to go through this,' I told him.

I wanted Lee to carry on talking but I was super conscious of the fact that this situation was completely out of my remit as a foster carer and I needed to call Patsy.

'I want you to keep talking to me but I need to let Patsy know what's happened,' I told him.

'I understand,' he nodded.

I didn't want to talk in front of Lee so I left him in the kitchen while I quickly went upstairs and called Patsy from my mobile.

'Something awful has happened,' I told her. 'Lee has just turned up on my doorstep. He's been badly beaten up and he says he was attacked by Brianna.'

'What?' she gasped.

Patsy listened as I explained what he had told me.

'I know I shouldn't have let him in but you should see the state of him, Patsy,' I said. 'He's in a mess and all normal procedure just went out of the window. I couldn't just tell him to go. He'd come to me for help and I couldn't not let him in.'

'Maggie, you did the right thing,' she told me. 'He obviously trusts you.'

While I was filled with panic, Patsy was very calm and logical.

'What we need to do first is take him to A&E and get him checked over to make sure nothing's broken or if he needs stitches,' she told me. She explained that she was currently at a meeting over an hour's drive away from the nearest hospital.

'I'm sorry to ask but would you be able to take him there?'

'Yes, of course,' I said.

It was mid-morning and it was several hours before I had to go and collect the children from school.

'I'll meet you there,' she told me. 'I'll be as quick as I can.'

'That's OK,' I told her.

'I'm also going to give the police a call and tell them what's happened,' she said. 'This sounds like a serious assault and I know they will want Lee to give a statement.'

'Do you think he will this time?' I asked. 'Remember how he panicked yesterday.'

'I think he'll have to,' replied Patsy. 'He can't dispute his injuries or what he's told you.'

I was anxious to get back to Lee and check he was OK. I was also worried that he might suddenly decide to leave and do a runner.

'I need to check on Lee now, but I'll see you at the hospital,' I told her.

'Take care, Maggie,' she replied.

I went downstairs where thankfully Lee was now slumped on the sofa. I couldn't stop myself from wincing when I saw his battered face again.

'I spoke to Patsy and she thinks it would be a good idea for me to take you to the hospital just to get you checked over.'

'No way,' snapped Lee. 'I'm not going to no hospital. I'm all right. I don't need to see no doctor.'

'Lee, you might have broken your nose or your cheekbone and I think you need to get that lip looked at. Please, just to be on the safe side. There's nothing to be embarrassed about.'

'All right,' he sighed.

I explained that Patsy was going to meet us there. I didn't tell him about her contacting the police yet as I was worried that he would get scared and run off. I would leave that for Patsy to talk to him about.

I helped him outside and into the car and we set off for the hospital. Lee had been through enough today so I didn't want to push him to answer any more questions. I just wanted to get him to A&E as quickly as I could.

In my own mind, I couldn't stop myself from second-guessing what was going to happen next, now we finally had a true picture of what had been going on.

Surely Lee couldn't go home to Brianna after what she had done to him? What would happen with the parenting assessment? What would be the impact of all of this on Bobby and the girls? There were so many things that needed to be worked out.

As we drove along, Lee suddenly turned to me.

'I'm not soft or stupid, you know,' he said. 'She trapped me without me realising that she was doing it, but then it was too late.'

'Lee, it's OK,' I soothed. 'Sadly, I think it's something that happens to a lot of men.

'I can see you're in pain and you don't have to talk to me if you don't want,' I added.

'I know I don't really know you, but I trust you,' he told me. 'I can see Bobby trusts you so I do too.'

'That's a real compliment,' I smiled. 'I think a lot of your son and I only want the best for him and for you.'

'Thanks,' he said.

Without any prompting from me, as we drove to the hospital, Lee started to open up about his relationship with Brianna.

'She was OK at first,' he said. 'She was funny and we had a laugh. I really fell for her and it all happened so fast. It was nice to have someone after being on my own for so long.

'She said she only ever wanted girls and she didn't like boys but I thought she would warm up to Bobby when she got to know him.'

He described how he hadn't realised that Brianna was isolating him.

'It was just little things at first, but then she made me delete my Facebook page and she didn't like me going out with my friends. She said it was because she didn't want me going off with someone else and I just thought she was the jealous type. I was flattered really that she cared so much about me.'

I didn't say anything and let Lee talk.

'I'm not the brightest tool in the box and I didn't pass no exams or nothing,' he continued. 'Bri said I was useless with money so she made me pay my benefits into her account. When I got the odd job here and there, I had to give the cash straight to her.

'Before I knew it, she was in control of everything. I weren't even allowed no bank card of my own. If I went to the corner shop even for a tin of beans, I had to give her a receipt to show her what I'd spent.

'Then when it was really bad, she took my phone away cos she said we couldn't afford it and she made me sleep on the floor.'

'Just like Bobby?' I asked and he nodded.

'She said I was weak and useless and didn't deserve to have a bed,' he sighed. 'By then, she'd worn me down so much, I truly believed it.

'By the time I realised what was happening, it was too late. Me and Bobby was trapped. I didn't think it could get no worse but then it got physical.'

It was horrific to hear. He described how Brianna would push him and hit him.

'I thought if I didn't fight back and took it, it would pass,' he admitted. 'But it didn't.'

I could see how hard it was for him to share this with me and I could see the shame that he obviously felt.

'Honestly, Lee, you don't have to tell me all of this,' I told him. 'You don't owe me any explanation.'

'I want to,' he said. 'I want you to understand why I didn't get me and Bobby out of there. I don't want you to think I'm a horrible person or a bad dad.'

'Lee, it's not for me to judge but I don't think you're a bad person.'

I felt like he should be sharing all of this information with the police and Patsy, not me. What if he denied everything again or had had enough when it came to them questioning him?

But as we drove, Lee seemed to want to share his story.

'The past six months it got really, really bad,' he said.

Hearing him describe what Brianna had done to him was absolutely horrendous. I gripped the steering wheel as he described how Brianna had threatened him with knives, bottles and a screwdriver.

'She'd goad me, tell me I was dumb, thick and useless,' he said matter-of-factly, staring straight ahead. 'She'd spit on me, scratch me, punch me and slap me when we were alone. But even though she was beating the living daylights out of me, I couldn't bring myself to hit her back,' he said. 'I just curled up in a ball on the floor to protect myself while she kicked me over and over again. She'd hit me in the head and give me black eyes and she burnt me with cigarettes.'

I remembered the red marks I'd seen on his wrist yesterday when Patsy was talking to him.

'She was clever,' he continued. 'If anyone saw my injuries she'd tell them I'd been in a fight so it looked like I was the aggressive one. She said if I ever told anyone, she would go to the police and say that I attacked her. She knew they'd believe her over me,' he said. 'Who would believe a nearly six-foot bloke was being terrorized by a five-foot something, blonde mum? 'Pathetic, eh?' He tried to laugh.

'She said if I ever grassed her up, they'd take Bobby away from me,' he said shaking his head. 'So you see I was trapped. We both was. We was trapped in hell with no way out.'

It was one of the most horrific things that I'd ever heard.

'I'm so sorry, Lee,' I sighed. 'No one deserves to be treated like that, but I'm so glad that you've told me the truth.'

I could see that it was a relief for him to finally share what had been going on.

Five minutes later, we pulled up in the hospital car park and I helped Lee into A&E. Thankfully it wasn't horrendously busy so we found a quiet spot in the corner. I got Lee sat down then I went to check him in at the desk.

I was sat next to Lee, filling in a form for him, when I saw Patsy rushing in through the entrance. As she walked over to us, her face dropped.

'Oh Lee,' she gasped. 'You poor thing. Maggie told me what happened.'

He looked mortified.

'I don't want to be here,' he blurted. 'I don't need no hospital.'

'No, Maggie did the right thing,' she replied. 'You need to be looked at.'

'Maggie, shall we go to the front desk and see if we can get a quiet room somewhere so we can all chat?' she suggested.

We walked to the desk and she pulled me to one side.

'Oh my God,' she gasped. 'She's really beaten him badly. I didn't think it would be that serious.'

'Honestly, Patsy, that's not the half of it,' I told her. 'He talked to me about it on the way here. That woman has made his and Bobby's lives a living hell.'

'Do you believe him?' asked Patsy. 'You don't think he could be making it up?'

'One hundred per cent,' I nodded. 'No one could make that level of detail up. Besides, I can see the burning shame and hurt in his eyes. He's completely traumatised.'

I also let Patsy know that I hadn't told Lee that the police would want to see him.

'I thought it was something that should come from you and I didn't want him to do a runner,' I said.

'I know it's highly unlikely, but I'll go and explain the situation to the front desk,' she said. 'I'll tell them the police are on their way and see if they've got a free room where we can all talk privately.'

I went back to sit with Lee. A few minutes later, Patsy returned and sat down with us.

'OK, while we wait for one of the doctors to examine you, Lee, they're going to let us wait in one of the X-ray rooms down the hallway that isn't being used at the moment.

'Lee, the police are on their way and it will give us all a quiet place to talk.'

Lee's face crumpled in panic.

'I don't want no police involved,' he blurted out. 'I can't do it.'

'Lee, you have to,' I told him. 'After everything you were telling me in the car, you have to report Brianna for this. She has made yours and Bobby's life a misery. She needs to be held accountable for that and punished.'

'I just want to go to sleep and never wake up,' he mumbled. 'I want it all to be over.'

'Lee, you can do this,' I told him. 'You've done the hard part. You've told us what's been happening. Brianna doesn't control you any more.'

I could see how exhausted he was.

It was another twenty minutes before two plain-clothed police officers arrived. For some reason, I'd expected it to be DC Orton, who had interviewed Bobby and both Brianna and Lee initially. The men explained they were from the Criminal Investigation Department.

One of them had grey hair and the other looked younger, maybe in his twenties.

'I'm DC Mick Fleming,' explained the grey-haired man. 'This is my colleague DC James Smythe.'

Patsy explained that the hospital had organised a room where they could go and chat.

'Lee hasn't been seen by the doctor yet but the staff know to come and find him there. His injuries take priority.'

'Of course,' said DC Fleming.

Lee looked panicked.

'Are we going to the room now?' he asked. 'Is Maggie coming with us?'

'Lee, I'm going to take Maggie to get a coffee while you chat to the detective constables,' Patsy told him. 'But I'll come and join you in a little while.'

'Don't worry, you're in safe hands,' DC Smythe told him.

Lee looked utterly terrified.

'There's nothing to worry about, Lee,' DC Fleming reassured him. 'I can see you've been through a lot today. We just need to ask you a few questions and take a couple of photos of your injuries.'

'It's going to be OK,' I reassured him. 'Just tell them the truth like you did to me.'

One of the receptionists behind the front desk came out to show them to the empty X-ray room. Patsy and I watched as Lee walked slowly down the corridor with them.

'Come on, let's go get a coffee from the vending machine,' Patsy told me. 'You look like you could do with one.'

'I could do with something stronger,' I joked.

My nerves were in tatters after the events of the past few hours.

'Thanks so much for everything you've done, Maggie,'

Patsy told me. 'It's great to see how much Lee trusts you. He obviously feels safe with you, like Bobby does.'

'I honestly couldn't believe it when he turned up on my doorstep in that state,' I said. 'It's just so awful. How could anyone treat someone like that?'

'You'd never guess it from looking at her,' replied Patsy.

Brianna was a small, pretty blonde woman and not someone you would expect to terrorize a grown man and his son.

'In fact, because of what Brianna said about him, I had Lee down as the aggressive, violent one,' she added.

I was still in total shock and disbelief that both father and son had suffered at the hands of this woman. I'd read about male domestic violence and I knew it went on but I'd never come across it before in my fostering. I knew it was more common than people thought, but many men were reluctant to speak out or seek help because of the stigma and their shame and embarrassment. Just like Lee had been.

'What's going to happen now?' I asked Patsy.

'Once the police have interviewed Lee and taken a statement, I'm assuming they will arrest Brianna and bring her in for questioning.'

She was now facing multiple allegations from child cruelty to possible Grievous Bodily Harm and assault.

'Once we know whether Brianna is going to be charged then we can take it from there,' she told me. 'We'll know more over the next few days.'

For now, while the police investigation was ongoing, all contact and the parenting assessments would be put on hold.

'What do I tell the kids?' I asked her.

'Nothing for the moment,' Patsy replied. 'I'll stay here and see what the doctors and the police say about Lee and I'll let you know what happens.'

After everything that had happened, I knew Lee definitely couldn't go back to the flat.

'Where will Lee go?' I asked.

'I'm not sure yet,' said Patsy. 'I'm going to get on the phone now and try and get him an emergency place in a hostel.'

I knew there wasn't much more I could do by staying at the hospital.

'I'm sorry to leave you, Patsy, but I'll have to go and pick the children up soon, and I need to nip home first,' I explained.

'No, you go,' she told me. 'Everything is under control here and I'll keep in touch with you when I know more.

'Don't worry, Lee and Bobby will be OK,' she reassured me. 'At least we know the truth now.'

'Yes,' I nodded.

As I drove home, I just felt desperately sad about the whole situation.

As soon as I got back, I called Becky and filled her in on what had happened.

'Goodness, Maggie,' she said. 'That's a lot for you to deal with.'

'Lee was in bad way,' I said. 'It's just horrendous to think what he and Bobby have been through.'

Then I had to go and pick the children up from school. It was hard to see Bobby and to think about how we were going to explain to him what had happened to his dad. Did he even know Brianna was hurting him too?

It wasn't until I was making dinner that Patsy called.

'Can you talk or are the kids within earshot?'

'No, it's fine,' I said. 'The girls are upstairs and Bobby's watching TV in the living room.'

She explained that Lee had given a statement to the police and they were going to question Brianna.

'How is he?' I asked.

'His injuries are a lot more serious than we thought,' she told me.

When the doctors examined Lee, it turned out that when he had curled up on the floor to protect himself, Brianna had kicked him.

'He's got some internal bruising and a broken rib,' she said. 'His forehead needed gluing and he needed stitches in his lip.'

They wanted to keep him in for a couple of days for observation.

'Poor guy. No wonder he was in so much pain,' I said.

She explained that Lee had asked for me to bring Bobby up to the hospital the following day.

'He wants to see Bobby himself and explain what happened,' she told me. 'He also wants to reassure Bobby that he's safe and also encourage him to tell the truth now. He wants him to know that Brianna can't hurt them any more.'

'But what do I say to him?' I asked. 'What do I tell the girls?'

'Please don't tell them anything at this stage,' Patsy told me. 'They can go to school as normal but I'm happy for you to keep Bobby off to visit Dad.'

My head was spinning. I wasn't sure how Bobby was going to take the news. Did he suspect anything already? Had he known that his dad was being abused by Brianna too? My mind whirred with questions that were yet to be answered. It was time for Bobby to know the truth.

TWELVE

No Going Back

As I tidied up the breakfast bowls, I casually dropped what would be happening into the conversation.

'Bobby, you and I have an appointment this morning so I'll take you back to school after that.'

'That's not fair,' moaned Melodie. 'Why do we have to go to school and he doesn't?'

'Bobby will be going back to school as soon as his appointment is over,' I told her firmly.

Bobby looked puzzled but he didn't say anything or ask me any questions about it.

It was only after we'd walked the girls to their classrooms and got back into the car that I heard a little voice from the back seat.

'What's my pointment?' he asked.

'It's called an a-ppointment,' I gently explained to him. 'And it's a meeting with someone. If you have an appointment with someone then you go and see them and this morning I'm taking you to see your daddy.'

Bobby looked surprised. I knew I needed to fill him in about what had happened and also to prepare him for how his dad might look.

'Am I seeing him at the centre?' he asked, but I shook my head.

'We're not going to the contact centre today, flower,' I replied. 'There's something I need to tell you about your dad, Bobby, but I don't want you to worry.

'Daddy got hurt and he's in the hospital, but he's going to be OK,' I explained. 'He wanted to explain that to you himself so you can see that he's going to be fine.'

Bobby nodded. I could see that he was taking it all in but thankfully he didn't ask what had happened to him. I felt any explanation needed to come from Lee himself.

Once we'd got to the hospital and I'd found somewhere to park, Bobby and I headed in through the main entrance. As we walked down the corridors searching for the ward Lee was on, I could see by the look on Bobby's face that he was apprehensive. I felt him reach for my hand and I gave it a reassuring squeeze.

'Ah, here we are,' I said as we finally saw a sign for Ward Six.

I paused just outside the double doors and crouched down so I was at Bobby's level.

'Dad's probably going to look a bit different than he does normally,' I told him. 'He's hurt his face and he's got some cuts and bruises but remember, the doctors are looking after him.'

He nodded.

'Does it hurt him?' he asked.

'He's in a little bit of pain but he's going to be OK,' I replied.

As a nurse directed us to Lee's cubicle, I could see that Bobby was very worried. There was a curtain around Lee's bed so I opened it slightly and peeked my head through. Lee was lying in bed with his eyes closed.

'Hi Lee,' I said gently and he stirred.

He looked worse than the day before. The gashes on his face had scabbed over, his lip had been stitched and had swollen up, and his eye was now purple.

'I've brought Bobby to see you like you asked,' I told him. 'We can come back in a little while if you're resting?'

'No, no, it's all right,' he told me, wincing in pain as he slowly sat himself up in bed. 'Bring the lad in.'

I pulled the curtain back and Bobby and I walked through.

'Hi son,' said Lee.

Bobby stared at the floor, not looking at his dad.

'Thanks for coming to see me.'

Bobby didn't say a word.

I moved a couple of chairs closer to Lee's bed.

'Let's sit down,' I suggested to him. 'Then you can have a chat to Daddy.'

As Bobby finally looked at his dad, I could see the shock on his little face.

'I look a mess, don't I?' Lee said to him and Bobby nodded.

'Don't worry son, it looks worse than it is.'

Things still felt stilted and awkward between Bobby and Lee and I knew if I didn't say anything, they would both probably just sit there in silence.

'Bobby, your dad would like to explain to you how he got hurt, wouldn't you, Lee?'

Now it was Lee's turn to look apprehensive. He couldn't make eye contact with him while he spoke.

'Brianna did this to me, Bobby,' he told him. 'She laid into me and hurt me. But I've told the police and Maggie what she's done and I want you to know that I ain't going to live with her no more. And you ain't either.'

Bobby didn't show any reaction at all. He just stared straight ahead.

'I know she hurt you too, Bobby, but you've gotta tell the truth now, son, because we're not going back there ever again. She can't hurt us no more. Do you understand?' he asked, and Bobby nodded.

Lee reached out across the bed to try and grab Bobby's hand but he quickly moved it.

'It's gonna be OK, son,' he told him.

Bobby was silent. I suppose he had never heard his dad speak out against Brianna before so it must have been confusing for him.

There was an awkward silence so I tried to break the ice and make conversation between them.

'Bobby will be going back to school later and he's doing so well, aren't you Bobby?' I smiled.

'That's good, son,' nodded Lee. 'What are your favourite lessons?'

Bobby shrugged.

'His teacher said he's really enjoying art and he's getting very good at maths too,' I told him. 'And his reading has really come on.'

'Is it son?' asked Lee. 'Well done.'

I wanted to give them something to talk about but I could see Lee was still tired and in pain and Bobby was desperately trying to process everything that he had just been told.

A few minutes later, Bobby pulled on my sleeve.

'Can we go now?' he whispered. 'I have to go to school.'

'OK,' I nodded.

I got up and moved the chairs back.

'Lee, we're going to leave now and get Bobby back to school but I've brought a few bits for you to keep you going while you're in the hospital,' I told him.

Lee looked like he was going to cry.

'Thanks so much,' he gasped.

'It's nothing fancy, just a few toiletries to tide you over,' I said.

I put a carrier bag containing a toothbrush and toothpaste, some deodorant, shaving gel and a packet of razors at the end of his bed.

'Can I have a hug, son?' Lee asked him.

Bobby shook his head and walked out of the cubicle.

'Give him time,' I told Lee and he nodded sadly.

We walked down the warren of corridors back towards the front entrance.

'How do you know where to go?' Bobby asked me in amazement.

'I've come here a lot over the years,' I told him. 'Down there is the children's ward and that's where I used to visit my daughter Louisa a long, long time ago, when she was in hospital.'

Bobby didn't say another word but I could tell by his serious face that he was going over everything in his mind.

It wasn't until we were in the car that he finally spoke.

'Maggie, we're not going to live with Brianna ever again, are we?' he asked.

'That's right,' I said. 'You and Daddy won't be going back to the flat.'

'Where am I going to live?

'Well at the moment you're going to stay living with me,' I told him. 'And Patsy is going to help Daddy find somewhere else to live.'

I decided to take Bobby to a café to get some early lunch before I dropped him back at school. He didn't say anything else until we pulled up into a car park in the centre of town.

'Will she get told off for hurting us?' he asked.

By 'she' I knew that he meant Brianna.

'The police are going to speak to Brianna and then they'll decide,' I told him. 'They will probably want to speak to you again too. This time, like Daddy said, you must tell them the truth. If Brianna did hurt you then you must tell them that.'

Bobby looked confused.

'But Melodie and Poppy are going to be really horrible to me if I tell,' he said.

'I can promise you I won't let them be mean to you or hurt you,' I reassured him. 'I'll make sure of that, so don't you worry.

'Patsy's not going to say anything to the girls at the moment,' I added. 'So they won't know anything that's happened unless you tell them. So let's wait until we know a bit more and then Patsy can speak to them.

'Don't worry,' I added. 'I know this is really hard for you and you're being so brave and we'll sort it all out. Patsy will tell you when any decisions are made, OK?'

He nodded.

When I glanced at my phone, I noticed there was a voicemail from Patsy. She was letting me know that DC

Orton had been in touch. In light of Lee's allegations, she wanted to re-interview Bobby.

While Bobby was choosing a sandwich at the café, I gave her a quick call back.

'If you don't think it's too much then why don't you take him to the police station this afternoon?' Patsy suggested. 'It might be better to get it all over and done with, in one day.'

'He seems OK after seeing Lee so perhaps it's worth a go,' I replied. 'Then he can go back to school as normal tomorrow.'

We would have enough time as the girls were at an afterschool club so they didn't need picking up until later on.

As we ate our lunch, I told him the new plan.

'Instead of going back to school this afternoon, I'm going to take you to see DC Orton,' I told Bobby as we tucked into a tuna sandwich.

'Remember she was the lady that you went to see ages ago when you first came to live with me?'

He looked puzzled.

'The one with the orange hair?' he asked.

'Well I'd call it red hair,' I smiled. 'But yes, that's the one.'

'Are we going to the place with the monster trucks again?' he asked me and I nodded.

All I could hope was that now Bobby had spoken to his dad, he knew he would never live with Brianna again and it was OK to tell the truth.

When lunch was over, we drove to the police station where Patsy was waiting for us at the entrance.

'Did you go and see Daddy at the hospital this morning?' she asked Bobby and he nodded.

'I bet he was really pleased to see you,' she smiled. 'He's feeling a lot better today.'

'Are you coming to see the lady too?' Bobby asked me.

'I'll come in with you, flower, but I won't be in the room with you this time as I have to make a couple of phone calls,' I told him. 'Patsy will be with you though, and DC Orton, and I'll be waiting outside for you. Do you think you can be a big brave boy and talk to them?'

He nodded.

Bobby had come on so much in his confidence in the past few weeks and I was worried that somehow my presence in the room would stop him from talking. I didn't want to do anything to jeopardise him from giving a statement.

Besides, what I had told him was true. I needed to call Becky as she'd asked me to keep her updated about what was going on.

There was a chair in the corridor, outside the interview room, so I sat on that and phoned her. I explained what had happened.

'Sounds like it's been a busy twenty-four hours,' Becky said.

'You can say that again,' I told her.

'Genuinely though, Maggie, how are you holding up?'

'I'm OK,' I said. 'The adrenalin is getting me through.'

A few things had been playing on my mind during all of this. As my supervising social worker, Becky was there to support me and I knew I could go through them with her.

'I think the girls and Bobby need to be separated,' I said. 'Once they know what's happening with Mum, it's potentially going to put Bobby in a very difficult situation and I think he's genuinely frightened of them.'

Regardless of what happened with Lee, if he and Brianna were not together then Bobby was never going to be returning to live with her. If he now admitted that Brianna had hurt him, and she wasn't a blood relation, he wouldn't have contact with her either. Who knows what would happen with the girls but, on the face of it, they had been well cared for by their mother. Whatever happened to the girls, I knew Bobby was unlikely to live with them again.

'I'll have a chat to Patsy and see what the plan is going to be moving forward but I think you're right about Bobby.'

It was all the unknown at the moment; I knew I just had to be patient and see how things unfolded.

After an hour, Patsy came out from the meeting room.

'I just wanted to nip to the loo,' she said.

'How's it going in there?' I asked.

'Bobby is doing so well,' she told me. 'DC Orton said to him that his dad had told them that it was Brianna who had hurt him and this time he admitted it straight away.'

'Bless him,' I said. 'He's being so brave. He must have been so frightened of her.'

'He said she wasn't very nice to him,' said Patsy.

'That's an understatement,' I sighed.

Hopefully now they had his taped interviews, this would be the last time that he'd have to be questioned.

'I don't think we'll be much longer,' Patsy told me. 'I can see Bobby's getting tired so I think they will call it a day soon.'

Patsy brought him out fifteen minutes later. He looked exhausted.

'Bobby did so well and answered all of DC Orton's questions,' she smiled.

'Are you OK, sweetie?' I asked him and he nodded.

'I got you this,' I said, handing him a bar of chocolate that I'd got from the vending machine. 'I thought you deserved a little treat.'

I knew it had been such a long, hard day for him.

Bobby was very quiet as we went to pick the girls up from school. Melodie pounced on him as soon as she got in the car.

'Why didn't you go to school today, Bobby? Where did you go?'

'Bobby just had an appointment but he'll be back in school as normal tomorrow,' I told her.

Bobby didn't say a word.

Sometimes after a day like today, kids needed a bit of time and space on their own just to chill out and decompress.

I put the telly on in the living room for him while I kept the girls busy with a pottery painting set that I'd found in my cupboard.

That night, I made sure he was in bed a little earlier than usual as I could see he was shattered.

'Night night,' I said, when I went to tuck him in. 'I know it's been a very hard day for you and you have been so brave.'

I ruffled his hair.

'And don't worry, your dad is getting better and he will be out of hospital very soon.'

I'd just turned out the light when I heard a voice in the darkness.

'I won't have to ever live with her again, will I?'

'No, you won't, lovey,' I told him. 'Brianna can't hurt you or Daddy any more. You're safe now.'

It broke my heart that he'd obviously been carrying round these worries for so long.

*

Thankfully Bobby slept well and I think he was almost relieved to go to school as normal the next morning after the events of the previous day. I got back from the school run and the supermarket to find Patsy on my doorstep.

'I was driving past your road so I thought I'd call in on the off chance that you were around,' she said.

'Of course,' I said. 'Come in and I'll put the kettle on.'

Even though it was just after 11 a.m., she already had updates.

'Brianna was arrested last night,' she told me.

They'd taken her to the police station to be questioned.

'And Lee was discharged from hospital early this morning.'

'Already?' I gasped. 'Where has he gone?'

Patsy had managed to find him a place in a hostel.

'I took him to the flat to collect his things,' she told me. 'We knew Brianna was in custody so it would be safe.'

Patsy described how he hardly had anything to bring. 'Just a couple of carrier bags and a tatty case. He didn't have much in the way of possessions. It's sad really.'

It reminded me of when Bobby had arrived at my house with his carrier bag.

'So what happens now?' I asked.

'As it stands, we don't know what's going to happen with Brianna,' she replied. 'We think it's likely that she's going to face more criminal charges of some sort and the police are going to keep me updated.

'What we do know is that whatever happens, Bobby isn't going to be living with Brianna or having any contact with her,' she continued.

She explained both the parenting assessment and contact had been put on hold between Brianna and the girls for the time being. Patsy had also managed to get in touch with their biological father and he was going to start having contact with the girls to see how that developed.

'Mike lives quite a long way away so it's not going to be that frequent but let's see how the first session goes,' Patsy explained. 'It's been years since they've seen him so we don't know how they will all get on.'

Patsy explained that their dad had also suffered at the hands of Brianna.

'When I explained what had happened, he wasn't surprised,' she told me. 'Brianna had been physically abusive to him during their marriage. Not to the same extent as Lee, but enough that he ending up leaving her.'

'If Brianna is charged and there's a chance she might get a custodial sentence, then we need to look at other long-term options for the girls. But what is clear is that we are dealing with two separate family units now – Lee and Bobby, and Brianna and the girls.'

I knew there was only one logical solution and it seemed that Patsy was thinking the same thing.

'Maggie, I think we need to split the girls and Bobby up,' she told me. 'And in my mind, the most logical solution is that we find a new foster carer for Melodie and Poppy, and Bobby stays with you.

'I know Bobby trusts you and you seem to have built up a rapport with Lee too.'

I was sad that the girls would be moving on but I knew that in reality it was the best plan.

'I agree with you,' I said.

Lee didn't pose a threat to Bobby so Patsy was happy for him and Bobby to keep having their contact sessions as long as they were supervised.

'I think we need to have another meeting to come up with the long-term plan,' she said. 'We need to see whether the police are going to charge Lee with anything and also help to get him a more permanent housing solution.'

'We don't even know at this point whether he wants Bobby back with him full-time. It might not be something that he feels he's able to cope with at the moment.'

It was all up in the air.

'What happens next then?' I asked.

'I'm going to try and find a new carer for the girls,' she said. 'Once we have someone lined up, we'll let the children know what's happening.'

'OK,' I nodded.

While I knew it was the right thing to do for everyone, I felt sad that the girls faced even more upheaval and another move. They were victims too in all of this and despite all of their talk and bravado, I knew how unsettling it would be for them.

'How long do you think it will take?' I asked.

'You know as much as me,' she said. 'It depends which carers have a vacancy.'

I knew from experience that it could be weeks but, more than likely, we'd be saying goodbye to the girls in a matter of days.

THIRTEEN

Moving On

As it turned out, everything happened very quickly. Patsy rang with an update the following morning.

'I've just had a phone call from DC Orton about Brianna,' she told me. 'She's been charged with Actual Bodily Harm against Lee and child cruelty in connection to Bobby.'

'Do we know if she's admitted it?' I asked.

'She hasn't issued a plea yet,' Patsy replied. 'There should be a hearing in court in the next few weeks.'

In the meantime, she'd been released on bail.

'Are the girls going to see her at contact?' I asked.

'Yes, we'll restart the sessions in a few days once they've moved to their new placement.'

'Oh, you've found someone already?' I gasped.

'Yes, I couldn't believe it either,' said Patsy. 'Luckily they just had a sibling group move on last week for adoption. You probably know them, Maggie, as you work for the same agency and they only live about fifteen minutes from you.'

She explained that it was a couple called Sue and

147

Derek. They were in their mid-fifties and had two grown-up daughters.

'Oh I know Sue,' I smiled. 'Yes, she's lovely. I've chatted to her at a few agency coffee mornings.'

She was a large lady with a big booming laugh and she was very warm and motherly. I'd never met Derek but I knew they'd been fostering for years, ever since their girls were tiny, so they were very experienced.

'The girls will be in safe hands there,' I agreed.

'What sort of timescale are you looking at to move them over?' I asked.

Patsy felt there was no benefit in waiting and I knew this sort of handover to a new carer was done pretty quickly.

'I thought I could come round tonight and talk to the girls after school,' she explained. 'Then tomorrow I could pick them up from school and take them to Sue and Derek's, then they could move the following afternoon.'

Wow, I thought to myself. So Melodie and Poppy would be gone in a couple of days.

'Obviously we'll need to explain to Bobby what's happening too,' she said. 'I'm happy for you to talk to him if that's easier.'

'Yes, I don't mind doing that,' I said.

I came up with a plan for that evening. I would have Bobby watching telly in the front room and then when Patsy arrived, I could take her through to the kitchen to talk to the girls. Then I would fill Bobby in on what was going on after Patsy had broken the news to them.

'Patsy's coming round in a little while to have a chat to you,' I told the girls as I got them a snack after school that afternoon.

Melodie rolled her eyes and Poppy showed no reaction.

I put the telly on for Bobby and told him the same thing.

'Oh, is she going to tell them about Brianna?' he whispered and I nodded.

'Don't worry, Patsy won't tell them that you've spoken to the police too,' I reassured him. 'We'll say that it's something Daddy has said.'

He nodded. The girls were still going to be around for the next couple of days and I didn't want him to be frightened.

When Patsy arrived ten minutes later, she popped her head around the door and said hello to Bobby. Then I took her through to the kitchen.

'Girls, come and sit at the table and talk to Patsy,' I told them. 'I've got you a juice and a biscuit each.'

Cue another eye roll from Melodie, but they did what I'd asked. Patsy chatted to them about school for a little while.

'Actually, I popped in today because I wanted to talk to you about your mum,' she told them. 'The police have been talking to Mum because we now know that she wasn't being very kind to Bobby and Lee and she was hurting them. Did you know that?'

Poppy looked at Melodie.

'Well, they shouldn't be so thick and do stupid things all the time,' Melodie sighed.

I couldn't hear her say something like that and not interrupt.

'Melodie, no one should be treated like that,' I told her firmly. 'Everyone deserves to be safe in their own home.'

'Well, I don't care,' said Melodie.

Then Poppy piped up.

'That's not very nice,' she told her sister. 'Maggie says it's good to be kind and that's not kind.'

'Oh, shut up, Poppy,' Melodie hissed.

I didn't blame Melodie; I knew her attitude and the way she spoke to Bobby and treated him was all learned behaviour from Mum. She didn't show any empathy because Brianna had never showed any towards Bobby or his dad. I was pleased that some of what I'd said was getting through to Poppy, but I knew there was still a lot of work that needed to be done with Melodie.

'Because of what has happened, Lee and your mum are not going to be living together any more,' Patsy continued. 'Bobby isn't going to be seeing your mum any more either.'

'Will we see Mummy any more?' asked Poppy in a quiet voice.

'Yeah, she weren't ever mean to us,' added Melodie.

'Yes, of course,' replied Patsy. 'We want you to keep on seeing Mummy and she wants to see you, so that's why we thought it was best for you both to move to a different foster carer to Bobby. Then you can still have contact with Mummy and still be safe but you wouldn't have to worry about what was going on with Lee and Bobby.'

'Oh that's really good,' smiled Melodie. 'Cos Maggie's really strict. I bet it will be really fun at our new house.'

Patsy ignored that comment and continued.

'We've found some lovely new foster carers who are going to look after you,' she told them. 'Their names are Sue and Derek and they live quite near to here. I'm going to pick you up after school tomorrow and we can go and visit them and see your new house.'

Both girls looked a bit stunned.

'But I like it here,' said Poppy.

'Don't worry, I bet it's gonna be a really nice house,' Melodie told her. 'Much nicer than here.'

'But where's Bobby going?' asked Poppy.

'Bobby's going to be staying here with me,' I told them.

'I'm glad we're leaving,' said Melodie firmly. 'This house is tiny.'

I didn't take offence at any of her comments. I'd seen it in children before. This was Melodie's way of mentally letting go and coping with moving on. It was easier to deal with if she convinced herself that she didn't like it here anyway.

Poppy looked a lot more apprehensive. I knew it was more change and upheaval for them.

'But I like it here,' she said quietly.

'You're going to really like your new house too,' I told her. 'I've met Sue and she's really lovely so I know she's going to look after you so well.

'And we will still see you. We'll be able to meet in the park and I'm sure we'll see each other at some other activities too.'

My fostering agency held regular fun days and events at Easter and Christmas and picnics over the summer where carers and their foster children got together. It was always nice to catch up with other carers and for the kids to all run round together.

'And of course, I'll see you at school when I'm picking Bobby up,' I smiled. 'So really, you're still going to be seeing lots of me.'

Melodie looked totally nonplussed.

While Patsy was telling the girls more about Sue and Derek, I went to speak to Bobby.

'I've got some news for you, flower,' I said, sitting down next to him on the sofa. 'Melodie and Poppy are going to go and live with another foster carer. They're going to stay with a very nice lady who I know called Sue, and her husband Derek.'

'Why?' he asked.

'Well, because Brianna hurt you, you won't be seeing her any more or live in the same house as her ever again,' I told him. 'But Brianna is still the girls' mummy and they want to see her so Patsy felt it was better for them to go and live somewhere else.'

'Will they live with her ever again?' he asked.

'I don't know at the moment,' I told him. 'We'll have to see what happens.'

He didn't say much. I thought he would be relieved to hear this news but he looked worried.

'What house am I gonna move to?' he asked.

'Oh lovey, I'm so sorry, I forgot to tell you that bit,' I smiled. 'You're not moving anywhere – you're going to stay here with me. Is that all right?'

He gave me a little smile and I patted his hand.

'I know it's a lot of change but I think it's for the best,' I told him.

Things would slowly start to work themselves out.

The rest of the evening consisted mainly of Melodie talking very loudly about how amazing it was going to be at their new house while Poppy and Bobby pushed their food around their plates in silence. I was trying to be upbeat, but I felt desperately sad for all three of them and the constant changes they were having to cope with. It was a lot for young children to deal with and I knew it must be so confusing for them. Even though their family had been unhappy, abusive and dysfunctional, they had still been part of that same family for the past couple of years.

When I tucked Bobby in that night, I could see there was something preying on his mind.

'This is still going to be my bedroom, isn't it?' he asked anxiously. 'Will I still have this bed?'

'This is definitely still going to be your bed in your bedroom and you'll be here tomorrow night and the night after that and the night after that and the night after that . . .'

Bobby laughed as I carried on.

'You'll always have a bed at my house,' I told him.

I could see that today's news had left him unsettled and he needed that extra reassurance.

I knew the new arrangement was going to take a lot of adjusting to for all of us. It was strange picking Bobby up from school the following day and not collecting the girls as well. Even Bobby asked where they were.

'Remember, they're visiting their new foster carers,' I told him and he nodded.

I really hoped it was going well and neither of them kicked up a fuss.

It was nearly seven o'clock. before Patsy dropped them back. Bobby was in the kitchen playing with some cars and I was glad that he was out of earshot when I asked them how it had gone.

'How was it?' I asked. 'Did you have a lovely time with Sue and Derek?'

I was being as upbeat as possible as I wanted them to see this move as a good thing.

'They were sooo nice,' said Melodie. 'The house is massive. It's really posh.'

'Me and Melodie have got our own bedrooms and they've got a telly in them,' added Poppy.

'Wow, that's brilliant,' I said. 'You're so lucky.'

'Their house is much bigger than yours and the bathroom is so much nicer,' said Melodie.

I'd actually been to Sue's house once before and I knew it was very similar to mine, but I gave Melodie a big smile.

'I'm so glad,' I told her. 'It sounds like a wonderful place and I think you're going to be really happy there.'

That night we needed to get their stuff packed as Patsy was going to take it over to Sue and Derek's the following day.

I knew when I dropped them off at school the next morning, it would be our goodbye.

I didn't want to make a big deal of it or create a scene, especially as Melodie and Poppy were going straight into school. It felt like a normal morning. The two suitcases by the front door were the only sign of what was going to happen later.

In fact, when we pulled up outside school, Melodie got out and started walking straight off to her classroom.

'Melodie, remember Patsy's going to pick you up from school and take you to your new house,' I told her. 'I'll give you a ring tonight to make sure that you've settled in OK. And of course you'll see Bobby at school tomorrow.'

She shrugged and walked off.

Poppy usually walked herself to her class too but today she hung back.

'Will you take me to my classroom?' she asked me.

'Of course I will,' I replied.

When we got to the door, I was surprised when she threw her arms around me.

'Bye bye, Maggie,' she said.

'I'll see you soon,' I told her and she nodded.

Bobby had been quiet through all of this and I had no idea what he was thinking.

'See you tonight, flower,' I said as I dropped him off at the door of his classroom.

He knew he would see the girls every day in school so I didn't want to force him to say goodbye. I knew it would be a huge relief for him not to have them around.

But as I drove home, I couldn't help but feel sad. I had a last check around the house for any of Melodie and Poppy's things before Patsy arrived to collect their suitcases. It was amazing how much stuff they had accumulated in just over a month.

'How did the goodbyes go this morning?' she asked me.

'It was fine,' I said. 'I tried not to make a big deal about it but I was surprised at how clingy Poppy was.'

'Yes, I think she's a sweet kid,' nodded Patsy. 'She's certainly a lot more empathetic than her sister.'

I helped Patsy load the cases into the boot of her car.

'I've arranged for Sue and Derek to collect the girls slightly earlier from school today,' she told me. 'I thought it might be confusing or upsetting for them if they bumped into you and Bobby at pick-up.'

'Good idea,' I said.

I must admit it did feel strange only picking Bobby up from school that afternoon.

'It's very quiet, isn't it?' he said in the car.

'It is,' I told him. 'But it's nice to be able to chat properly to you.'

Rather than go home to an empty house, I wanted to do something different.

'I thought we could go round to Louisa's for tea,' I said. 'Would you like that?'

It made such a difference having one child rather than three and it meant that we could do things like this. Bobby had met Louisa a couple of times and I'd given her a heads-up about what had happened.

He nodded.

'Will the baby be there?' he asked.

'Yes, Edie will be there,' I smiled. 'But she's more of a toddler now than a baby.'

It was a nice distraction being at someone else's house. Louisa made a fuss of Bobby and he loved playing with Edie.

'What a sweet little lad,' she told me.

'He is,' I said.

It was nice to see that he had the confidence to chat to Louisa.

'The other day we went to the hospital that Maggie said you were in,' he told her.

She looked at me quizzically as if to ask why he had been in the hospital.

'His daddy was in hospital and we went to visit him and we walked past the children's ward,' I told her. 'And I told Bobby how you were there once.'

'Yes, that was a long, long time ago,' she told him.

We were back home by six-thirty. It felt strange, walking into the house and not seeing the girls' things around us. Little things that I was so used to seeing, like their purple school bags by the front door and their pink coats hanging on the banister. I could see Bobby was tired so I ran him a bath. While he watched TV afterwards, I gave Becky a quick call.

'How did it go today?' she asked.

'Oh, it was fine,' I said. 'I didn't make a fuss and the girls seem to be dealing with it OK. I think it's a relief for Bobby.'

'That's good,' she replied.

There was something else on my mind that I wanted to talk to Becky about. Normally, when a child or children left, it would only be a matter of days before a new placement arrived to fill that space. Sadly there were never enough foster carers to cope with the large numbers of children in the care system. Sometimes I'd got a new placement lined up even before a child had physically left and now that the girls were no longer with me I had the space to take on another two or even three children in the other bedroom.

'I wondered if you'd mind waiting a bit before you put me back on the "available list",' I told her.

'Yes of course,' she replied. 'That's completely up to you.'

'Just give me a couple of weeks,' I said. 'After everything that's happened to Bobby, I think he really needs some one-to-one time and attention.'

'No problem,' Becky replied. 'I won't put you forward for any other placements. You just tell me when you're ready.'

I knew it was the right thing to do. Bobby had been through so much – physically and psychologically. Now the girls had gone, the next few weeks were all about healing and helping to build up his self-esteem and confidence. After years of abuse, it wasn't going to be easy or instant, but I was going to give it a damn good try.

FOURTEEN

Freedom

Rain lashed down the window as Bobby and I snuggled up under a blanket on the sofa.

'I'm so glad we didn't go to the park,' I sighed. 'We would have got soaked.'

Instead, I'd made us a bowl of popcorn and we were watching the telly. Sometimes, nothing beats a lazy day on the sofa on a bleak winter's day!

I'd let Bobby choose what we were watching and a children's drama series was on. There was a scene where a little girl was having a birthday party and she and her friends were playing musical statues. I glanced over at Bobby and he had a strange look on his face.

'Bobby, are you enjoying this or shall we put something else on?' I asked him. 'You're looking very confused.'

'I've done statues but it wasn't like this,' he said, his eyes glued to the screen. 'This wasn't the statues I know.'

'Tell me about the statues you know then,' I asked him. 'Did you play it at a party?'

Bobby shook his head.

'No, Brianna made me do it,' he replied.

I listened, much to my horror, as he went on to describe how, as a punishment, Brianna had made him stand holding his hands above his head.

'How long did you have to stand like that?' I asked him.

'For a long, long time,' he sighed. 'My arms went all tingly and hurt, but if I put them down, she kicked me.'

'Did it happen a lot?' I asked him and he nodded.

It was absolutely horrific and I had to blink back the tears in my eyes as I didn't want Bobby to see me cry. I'd heard about so-called stress positions that were used in some countries as corporal punishment and as a method of torture. It was unbearable to think how painful it must have been for him to have to stand like that for God knows how long.

'Bobby, I'm so sorry that you had to do that,' I told him. 'That's not right and it shouldn't have happened. That's a very mean thing for an adult to put you through.

'Did Brianna make you do anything else?' I asked gently.

He described how sometimes he had to kneel on a hard floor for hours.

'Were the girls there when you had to do this?' I asked and Bobby nodded.

'I wet my pants cos I couldn't move and Melodie laughed.'

'Gosh, you must have been there for a very long time,' I said, taking his hand. 'It's no wonder that happened.'

I tried to reassure him that it was OK and understandable; I didn't want him to feel any shame about it.

'I wish I could change the past, Bobby, but I can't,' I told him. 'All I can say is that I promise you that no adult will ever make you do something like that again. You're safe now, OK?'

He nodded but I wasn't sure if he quite believed it. It helped me to understand why he found it difficult to trust Lee as everything he had been through had taught him that adults couldn't be trusted.

Although it was heartbreaking to hear these things, what was even more distressing was the matter-of-fact way Bobby recounted them. This horrendous abuse had been an ordinary part of his day-to-day life. It was horrifying to know that he'd suffered this way and been subjected to such cruelty on a regular basis.

That evening I knew I needed to make sure that everything Bobby had told me was typed up in my daily notes that I sent to Patsy and Becky. A foster carer's notes could be submitted to a court as evidence so I knew that they needed to be very factual and without emotion just in case they were needed by the police to help build a case against Brianna.

As we sat huddled up under our blanket, Bobby chatted some more.

'I like this house now Melodie's not here cos she can't get me into trouble no more,' he told me.

'But I don't think she ever got you into trouble here, did she?' I asked.

'No, but she did in my old house,' he replied.

'What kinds of things did she do?' I asked.

Bobby described how he was hungry one day so he'd taken a handful of crisps from the cupboard when Brianna was in the shower.

'Melodie told on me and I got hit,' he said. 'That's not kind is it, Maggie?'

'No, it's not,' I agreed.

'Was Poppy mean to you too?' I asked but, to my surprise, Bobby shook his head.

'Poppy was kind sometimes when Melodie wasn't around,' he replied. 'She sneaked me a biscuit if I was really starving hungry. And sometimes when Brianna made me do the kneeling, Poppy got me a blanket so my knees didn't hurt no more.'

'That was a nice thing to do,' I nodded. 'It sounds like Poppy looked out for you.'

'Yes,' he nodded. 'Poppy was my friend.'

I was surprised to hear this. I hadn't noticed that Bobby and Poppy had a relationship, probably because Melodie had always been around and had dominated things.

A few days after Melodie and Poppy had left, Patsy called.

'How are things without the girls?' she asked.

'It's fine,' I said. 'The house does feel quiet without them but I think Bobby's enjoying the one-to-one attention.'

'I've been reading your notes,' she told me. 'It's heartbreaking to hear everything he went through.'

'I know,' I replied. 'He's really opening up about things now he knows that he and Dad are safe, and he's allowed to talk.'

Patsy told me that she'd passed all of my notes about the abuse to the police.

'I'm not sure if he mentioned these incidents in any of his police interviews so they might want to speak to him again,' she said.

I didn't want Bobby to have to go through that again but I appreciated that they may have to re-interview him.

'I was actually ringing you about Lee,' said Patsy. 'I've been trying to sort out contact.'

She explained that now the sessions had been split between Bobby and the girls, she was struggling to find an available slot at the contact centre.

'Lee wants to see Bobby and I'm conscious that they haven't seen each other since Lee was in the hospital,' she told me. 'So I wondered if you would mind taking Bobby to meet him in the park one afternoon after school? It would just be for half an hour or so and you would be there with them to supervise.'

'Yes of course,' I said. 'I'm happy to do that.'

I knew that both Bobby and Lee would probably prefer that to meeting at the contact centre. Sessions there always felt very unnatural and forced as parents and children often felt like they were being watched and judged by the contact workers and it never felt very relaxed.

'Great,' said Patsy. 'I'll get that organised with Lee.'

We arranged to meet Lee a couple of days later in a park close to the hostel where he was staying. I took Bobby there after school but it was a bitterly cold February afternoon and I knew we'd only have until five before it started getting dark.

Lee was already waiting there when we pulled up into the car park. He was wearing a cap but I could see his face was still very bruised and swollen.

'How are you doing?' I asked him.

'Getting there,' he shrugged. 'My eye's been every colour of the rainbow.'

Bobby huddled behind me and didn't say a word to his dad.

'Lee, why don't you take Bobby on to the playground?' I suggested.

'OK,' he replied.

He and Bobby walked to the playground in silence. As soon as he pushed open the little metal gate, Bobby ran off to the slide. Lee just stood around watching while Bobby went on the slide, the climbing frame and the roundabout. I went over and stood with Lee.

'I don't think Bobby wants me around,' he sighed.

'Did you ask him if he wanted you to push him on the swing or spin him on the roundabout?' I suggested.

'No, but I don't think he'd let me,' Lee replied defensively. 'He doesn't want anything to do with me.'

Things still felt very forced and awkward between them.

'Give him time,' I said. 'You've both been through a lot. You have to forge a new relationship without Brianna around and you're going to have to win his trust.'

I knew Lee needed to learn to be around his son too and work at establishing that bond.

'How's the hostel?' I asked him.

'Grim,' he said. 'It ain't no place for a kid. I wouldn't want Bobby around most of the fellas in there.'

It was the first time that I'd heard Lee acknowledge that he wanted Bobby with him.

'Is that what you'd like to happen?' I asked him. 'Do you want Bobby to live with you full-time?'

'Yeah, course,' he said. 'I want to get my boy back. I want to make it up to him.'

'Have you talked to Patsy about that?' I asked him and he nodded.

'She says they're gonna have a meeting and then they'll decide,' he said. 'Maybe they'll have to do one of those assessments with me?'

'They will probably want to do a parenting assessment,' I nodded. 'You'll need to get somewhere permanent to live.'

'Yeah, Patsy said she'll help me put my name down for a flat,' he replied.

I couldn't help but wonder whether going to live with his dad was something that Bobby wanted too. I knew Lee was also waiting to hear from the police about whether he was going to face any charges for failing to prevent Brianna from abusing Bobby. There were so many things still to be worked out.

It was freezing standing around watching Bobby in the playground and he and Lee weren't really spending time together.

I walked over to Bobby, playing on the monkey bars.

'Why don't we go with Dad and get a cup of tea in the café?' I suggested to him.

We found a table and I left Lee and Bobby there while I went to the counter to get us some drinks. As I walked back over to them with a tray, I could see they were both still sitting there in silence.

'Here we go,' I smiled, putting down two cups of tea and a hot chocolate.

'Bobby, why don't you tell your dad about what you've been doing at school,' I suggested, desperate to encourage some interaction between the pair of them.

'Reading,' shrugged Bobby. 'And maths and science.'

'Oh, do you like science?' asked Lee. 'I wasn't no good at school but I liked science.'

'It's fun,' nodded Bobby. 'I liked it the other day cos we did electricity circuits.'

He described how they'd plugged lots of wires into a battery and it had made a little light bulb go on.

'That sounds good,' smiled Lee. 'I think I remember doing that when I was at school.'

It was nice to see them chatting at last. It didn't come naturally yet but they just needed a little help getting there.

'Well, I think it's time Bobby and I headed back now,' I told Lee when we'd finished our drinks. 'I need to get dinner in the oven.'

We walked out to the car park together.

'See you, son,' said Lee.

'Bye,' said Bobby awkwardly, shuffling his feet.

Lee leant over to hug him but Bobby quickly ducked out the way and ran back towards the car. I could see the rejection on Lee's face.

'He hates me,' he sighed.

'No, he doesn't,' I told him. 'He just needs to learn to trust you again. Give him time.'

But as Lee walked off, I could feel his disappointment.

I didn't mention anything to Bobby and I would never ever force a child to be affectionate towards any adult, even their birth parent. It had to be their decision and on their own terms.

I knew that contact could be very tiring for children. In the fostering world, there has been a lot of discussion about whether contact with birth parents sometimes actually retraumatises children and does more harm than good. The argument is that it's taking them out of an environment that is positive and putting them back into an environment that is negative.

I think it depends on the parents and the reason the child came into the care system in the first place. In some cases, I do think contact three times a week can be too much for kids. However, in Bobby's case, it was important that he had regular contact with Lee so they could start to rebuild their relationship.

The following day was Saturday and I had a plan up my sleeve.

'We're doing something very exciting today,' I told Bobby. 'Louisa and Charlie are going to a wedding so we're looking after Edie.'

'Will she stay for a long time?' he asked.

'Yes, she'll be here all day,' I nodded. 'We'll give her lunch and dinner and we might even take her to a farm. Would you like that?'

Bobby nodded excitedly. He waited patiently by the front window so he could see when Louisa and Charlie's car pulled up.

'They're here!' he yelled, racing to the front door.

When Edie toddled in, Bobby wrapped his arms around her. 'Hello baby Edie,' he said. 'Let's go and play with some toys.' He grabbed her hand and led her off into the kitchen.

'He's such a sweet boy,' Louisa smiled as she handed me a bag of things for Edie. 'Thanks so much, Maggie.'

'No problem, we'll love having her,' I told her. 'You two go off and enjoy yourselves.'

Bobby was in the kitchen with Edie showing her all of the toys. He was so caring with her and was constantly checking with me that she was OK.

'What time is her mummy coming to get her?' he asked. 'They will come back and get her, won't they?'

'Course they will sweetie,' I reassured him. 'They'll be back in time to put Edie to bed tonight, don't you worry.'

I often found that children who had been physically abused were very protective over little ones. They have this innate desire to protect others, perhaps because they haven't been protected themselves.

That afternoon we took Edie to a little petting farm about half an hour's drive from my house. There were rabbits, chickens, goats and sheep and she loved it.

'Wabbit,' she said, pointing.

'Good girl, Edie,' Bobby told her. 'It is a rabbit.'

She ran off towards the hutches but suddenly she tripped and fell over on the gravel. She let out an ear-piercing howl as she lay sprawled on the ground. Bobby looked horrified.

We dashed over to her and I picked her up and had a look at her knee.

'Oh, you're fine,' I said. 'Nana will make it better.'

I gave Edie's knee a gentle rub then I wrapped my arms around her and gave her a cuddle.

'All better now,' I smiled.

The tears quickly stopped and she ran back off towards the hutch to see the 'wabbit'. I could see Bobby watching all of this with interest.

'She forgot about the hurt so quickly,' he said in amazement.

'I think she forgot quickly because she knows there's always someone there to rub her knee and give her a cuddle.'

I paused.

'Did you not want to cuddle your daddy when we saw him yesterday?'

Bobby shrugged.

'Daddy doesn't really want to cuddle me. He didn't cuddle me when we lived with Brianna.'

I could see the hurt in his eyes.

'I think Daddy was probably frightened of Brianna and I think he knew Brianna would get cross with him if he cuddled you,' I told him.

'But now it's just you and Daddy, you can cuddle each other whenever you like.'

Bobby didn't look convinced.

'I don't want to,' he said firmly. 'Daddy was naughty.'

My heart sank.

'Why?' I asked. 'What did he do?'

'If someone's being nasty and they're a bully then my teacher says you have to tell on them. Daddy knowed that Brianna was being nasty to me but he didn't tell on her.'

It was such a complicated situation to explain to a child.

'I know it's really difficult to understand, Bobby,' I told him.

'Brianna was hurting Daddy too and he was so scared of her, just like you were, so he didn't tell anyone either.

'He's going to do better now because Brianna isn't in your lives any more and she will never hurt you and Daddy again,' I added.

It was about making him realise that they were both victims and Lee was hurting too. I could see Bobby didn't trust Lee yet and I completely understood. His dad should have been there to protect him but he wasn't. In his eyes he'd been hurt and his dad had been there and done nothing. It was no wonder he felt let down.

★

On Monday, I was picking Bobby up from school when I saw a blonde-haired woman waving at me in the distance.

'Oh, there's Sue,' I said, giving her a wave.

'Who's Sue?' asked Bobby.

'It's the lady who Melodie and Poppy are living with,' I told him.

I would have thought that I would have bumped into her sooner but it was the first time that I'd seen her on the school run. It was also the first time that I'd seen Melodie and Poppy since they'd left although I knew Bobby saw them at school most days.

'Hi girls,' I said, going over to them.

'Hello,' smiled Poppy shyly.

'It's so nice to see you, Maggie,' beamed Sue. 'I've been meaning to give you a ring.'

'How's it going, girls?' I asked them.

'Brilliant!' Melodie exclaimed. 'Come on, Sue, let's go to the shop and get some sweets.'

'Melodie, you know we don't get sweets on a Monday,' Sue told her. 'That's a Friday treat.'

I could see Melodie was trying to show off in front of me and Bobby.

'Well, I'm glad you're settling in, girls, and hopefully we'll bump into you again soon,' I told them.

As they walked off, Poppy turned round and gave me a little wave.

The following morning, I got a phone call.

'Maggie, it's Sue,' said a voice. 'I hope you don't mind me ringing you – I asked Patsy for your number.'

'No, not at all,' I replied. 'I meant to say when I bumped into you yesterday, ring me if I can help with anything. How are the girls doing?' I asked.

'Poppy's a sweetheart,' replied Sue. 'But I'm finding Melodie quite difficult and she can be very cruel to Poppy. She's always picking on her.'

I explained that Melodie had always been like that with Bobby.

'Perhaps now Bobby's not around, Poppy is an easy target?' I suggested.

We talked about how all Sue could do was pull her up on it and she would learn her actions had consequences.

'She'll eventually learn that you don't treat people like that,' I said.

We also talked about if any long-term plans had been worked out for the girls.

'They've restarted contact with Mum but the parenting assessment has been put on hold until they know what's happening with the courts,' Sue told me.

It wasn't breaching confidentially to talk about the girls with Sue because we were colleagues. I saved her number on my phone and told her to ring me whenever she needed to chat. Even though the girls had left my house, I still cared about what happened to them and I wanted the best for them.

A few days later, I'd picked Bobby up from school and we'd been to the supermarket. As a special treat, we'd popped in and got a McDonalds on the way home.

We'd just got in the car and I was about to start the engine when my phone rang.

I glanced down and saw Sue's name flash up on my phone. Something made me pick it up.

'Maggie, something's happened,' gasped Sue. 'Poppy's gone missing.'

'What do you mean by missing?' I asked.

I could hear the panic in Sue's voice as she explained that they lived in a cul-de-sac that had a small playground at the end of it.

'It's only two houses away from us so I can practically see it from my house,' she said. 'I've let Melodie and Poppy go on their own a couple of times, just for five or ten minutes while I got dinner sorted.

'Poppy and Melodie asked to go out after school today,' she continued. 'Derek was weeding the front garden so he was checking on them. But Poppy was there one minute and the next she was gone.'

Her voice cracked with emotion.

'Melodie said she didn't know where she was and there's no sign of her in the street. Derek's knocking on doors now just to check she hasn't gone back with another child.'

'Have you phoned Patsy?' I asked.

'I've tried her a couple of times and had to leave a voicemail,' she said. 'I'm about to ring the police. I wanted to check with you first to see if you had any idea about where she might have gone.'

I racked my brains.

'I honestly don't know,' I sighed. 'Do you think maybe she's tried to go back to her old flat to see Brianna?'

'I did think that,' said Sue. 'I'll talk to Patsy about that when I get through to her.'

But their old flat was nearly an hour away from Sue's house and I knew Poppy would have no idea how to get herself there.

'It's nearly dark, Maggie. I'm so, so worried.'

I explained that I was just on my way home.

'You're only round the corner from me,' I told her. 'Do you want me to drive around and look for her?'

'If you don't mind, that would be so helpful, Maggie,' she said. 'Thank you.'

'I just need to quickly drop my shopping home then I'll be right with you,' I told her.

As soon as I got off the phone, I knew Bobby would ask me what was going on.

'Sue can't find Poppy but don't worry, there are lots of people looking for her so we'll find her, OK?'

Bobby looked scared but he nodded.

As I drove us back to my house, I felt my heart pounding in my ears. It was a foster carer's worst nightmare as much as a parent's when a child disappeared on your watch. I could understand Sue's panic as the same thing had happened to me in the past.

Years ago, I'd had two foster children who'd gone to a park that was a stone's throw from my house. They were eleven and thirteen at the time and even though I'd given them strict instructions to come straight back, they'd decided on a whim to walk the five miles into town. Filled with utter panic when it got dark and they hadn't come home, I'd reported it to my social worker and the police. Officers ended up picking them up on the main road an hour later. It had honestly felt like the longest hour of my life so I knew exactly what Sue was going through.

When I pulled up outside my house, I turned to Bobby.

'You wait in the car while I take the shopping in, then we'll head straight to Sue's,' I told him.

He looked so worried, bless him.

I hooked three bags over each arm and staggered up the front path. I put them on the floor while I fumbled for my keys in my bag in the darkness. I pushed the keys into the lock, opened the door and flicked the hall light on.

Only then did I see her. A tiny figure crouched down in the darkness by the bush near my front door.

Poppy.

FIFTEEN

Finding His Voice

'Poppy!' I gasped. 'What on earth are you doing here?'

I could see from her bloodshot eyes that she'd been crying and she was shaking with cold.

'Come on,' I said gently, putting my arm around her and helping her up off the icy ground. 'Let's get you inside.'

I led her through to the kitchen and got her sat down.

'Give me two minutes while I get Bobby from the car,' I told her.

I dashed outside and brought him in.

'Poppy's in the kitchen,' I told him. 'You go and see her while I quickly call Sue.'

He looked at me quizzically but there was no time to explain. I needed to let Sue know that Poppy was safe.

Sue picked up on the first ring.

'Poppy's here at my house,' I told her. 'She was on the doorstep when I got back.'

'Thank God! What a relief! Why did she go to your house?'

'I honestly don't know,' I told her. 'I got her inside and phoned you straight away so I haven't had a chance to talk to her yet.'

'I'd better phone Patsy and let her know not to call the police,' said Sue. 'Then I'll come and get her.'

'There's no rush,' I replied. 'Let Patsy know and I'll keep Poppy here, get her warmed up and we'll have a chat.'

'Thanks so much, Maggie,' she told me.

When I went back inside, Poppy and Bobby were sitting in the kitchen in silence. I went over to her.

'What happened, lovey?' I asked. 'What are you doing here? Sue was worried sick when you disappeared from the playground.'

'I wanted to come and see you and Bobby,' she said, her voice quivering.

Then she burst into tears.

'It's OK, Pops,' said Bobby, patting her leg.

'Of course you can come and see us but you needed to ask Sue about it and her and Patsy could have arranged it,' I told her. 'Everyone was so worried about you.'

While I put the kettle on to make her and Bobby a hot chocolate, I thought what a miracle it was that Poppy had managed to find her way from Sue and Derek's house to here. She'd done the route in the car a few times but it was a good fifteen to twenty-minute walk. It was odd that she had suddenly decided to go walkabout and it was very out of character for Poppy, who was normally glued to Melodie's side.

'Are you sure everything's OK, Poppy?' I asked again as I put a mug of steaming hot chocolate on the table next to her. 'Did something happen?'

Poppy buried her head in her hands and started to cry again.

'I heard Sue talking to Patsy on the phone and she said Mummy's going to go to prison,' she sobbed. 'Is that true?'

'Oh flower,' I soothed, smoothing her long brown hair behind her ears. I couldn't tell her that it wasn't true because the likelihood was that Brianna would indeed get a custodial sentence.

'No one knows what's going to happen just yet,' I told her. 'Mum does have to go to court for how she treated Bobby and Lee and then it's up to a judge to decide. But whatever happens, you'll still be able to see her.'

Poppy nodded.

'But where will we live if she goes to prison?' she asked with big, sad eyes. 'Will we have to stay at Sue's forever? Where will Bobby go?'

'No one knows yet,' I told her. 'Lots of decisions need to be made first. But for now you and Melodie will stay with Sue, and Bobby will stay here with me, and Patsy will make sure that she tells you everything that's happening.

'I know it's hard, lovey, but lots of people care about you and your sister and Bobby and we'll all do our very best to make sure you're OK.'

Poppy nodded. It's so difficult when you can't give children a definitive answer about what's going to happen to them but in my opinion it's even harder if you lie. Sometimes you just have to be honest and say that you don't have the answers.

My phone suddenly vibrated with a message. It was from Sue.

On my way over now.

'Sue will be here in a minute,' I told her. 'So you have a chat to Bobby and I'll go and let her in.'

They drank their hot chocolates while I went to open the front door just in time to see Sue pull up outside. She rushed up the path.

'Thanks so much, Maggie,' she gasped. 'How is she?'

'She's cold but thankfully she's OK,' I replied.

'Has she said anything about why she came here?' she asked.

'I think she wanted to see Bobby and she was upset because she heard you on the phone to Patsy talking about Brianna going to prison.'

Sue's face fell.

'Oh gosh, poor girl,' she sighed. 'I thought she was in the other room watching telly. I can't believe she heard that – I should have been more careful.'

'Don't beat yourself up about it – these things happen,' I said.

'I think it's been a really unsettling few weeks for her and that was probably the final straw,' sighed Sue.

She explained that the girls had just started having contact with their biological dad, Mike.

'He lives quite a distance away so it's only going to be once a fortnight at first,' she said. 'I think it's going to take a while for them to establish a relationship with him. It's all still very new.'

Sue described how Melodie had been misbehaving at school but, on the surface, Poppy had seemed fine.

'She's obviously taking it all in and worrying about the future,' she said.

'The main thing is, she's safe,' I smiled. 'She's had a hot chocolate so she's warmed up a bit now.'

I took her through to the kitchen.

'Poppy!' said Sue. 'You gave me such a fright but I'm glad you're OK.'

'Sorry,' she said sheepishly.

'Let's get you back to my house,' she added.

'I was thinking, Poppy, if Sue was OK with it, perhaps you could come over for tea one night and see Bobby?' I suggested. 'I could pick you up from school.'

'That would be nice, if you wanted to?' Sue said and Poppy nodded.

'Will Melodie be coming?' asked Bobby anxiously.

'No, flower, it would just be Poppy,' I reassured him.

I hadn't realised up until now that Poppy and Bobby actually had a positive relationship. It was only really apparent when Melodie wasn't around but it was nice to think that they had looked out for each other. Even though they weren't biological siblings, they'd been part of the same family for two years and it was good for them still to be in each other's lives.

One afternoon I was filling in some school permission forms when I noticed the date of birth on them.

'Bobby, I've just realised that it's your birthday next month,' I told him. 'You're going to be nine.'

'Am I?' he asked.

'Yes,' I smiled. 'In two weeks. Would you like to have a little party? You could invite some of your friends from school if you wanted.'

'Oh, do you do boy's birthdays?' he asked, sounding surprised.

'What on earth do you mean?' I smiled. 'We celebrate everybody's birthday in this house.'

'I wasn't allowed no birthdays at my old house,' he replied. 'Brianna said only girls were allowed to have birthdays.'

I couldn't believe what I was hearing.

'So what did you do on your birthday?' I asked.

'Nothing,' he shrugged. 'I didn't know when it was. I think Dad whispered it in my ear one time and said "Happy Birthday" but I didn't have nothing else.'

'Did Melodie and Poppy celebrate their birthdays?' I asked and Bobby nodded.

'I wasn't allowed to do join in though,' he sighed. 'I had to do statues in my room when they were doing their birthday.'

Birthdays weren't about expensive presents, cakes or parties, it was just about acknowledging it and making children feel special. Denying a child the chance to mark their birthday is giving them the message that they're not worth celebrating. I was determined to try and change that for Bobby.

'Well we definitely celebrate boys' birthdays in this house,' I told him. 'So let's come up with a plan.'

The main things I knew I had to work on with Bobby were his self-confidence and self-esteem. Over the past few years, his dignity and self-worth had slowly been destroyed by Brianna's physical and emotional cruelty. If you're constantly told that you're useless and worthless and nothing you do is ever good enough, then you start to believe it.

I knew my job now was to build that back up in Bobby. I wanted to make him feel like he was worth something, that he deserved to love and be loved and that he *was* good enough.

I could see it in the way that he had no expectations. Bobby never asked for anything or expected anything to be for him.

I went to the supermarket one day and saw a little LEGO monster truck set that was reduced to half price.

I know who will love that, I thought to myself.

When we got home from school that afternoon, I handed Bobby the supermarket bag.

'I got this today,' I smiled.

He opened the bag and pulled out the box. Then he looked at me, puzzled.

'Who's this for?' he asked.

'It's for you, flower,' I told him.

'Why did you buy this for me?' he replied.

'Because I saw it when I was doing the shopping and I thought you would like it.'

Bobby stared at the box of LEGO.

'Is it a trick?' he asked.

'What do you mean, a trick?' I said.

'Brianna used to give me stuff like food or toys then she'd take them off me and say it was really for the girls and I wasn't allowed it.'

Poor lad. All I could do was reassure him.

'Bobby, I'd never ever trick you,' I told him. 'That would be cruel. There's nobody else living in my house and the only person I bought this LEGO for is you.'

I could tell Bobby still didn't believe me. He sat for ages just holding the box and staring at it. Then he put it down on the bedside table in his room.

He did the same the next night after school.

On the third night, Bobby still hadn't opened the box.

'Why don't you have a go at that LEGO I got you?' I suggested.

'Are you sure it's mine?' he asked again. 'If you wanna take it back I don't mind.'

'It's a present for you, lovey, and it's yours to keep,' I repeated. 'No one is going to take it away from you. I want you to build it and enjoy it.'

In the end, we ended up building it together. Bobby couldn't believe or trust that someone had bought something just for him.

I was constantly looking for ways to boost Bobby's self-confidence day-to-day. One morning, ABBA's song 'Dancing Queen' came on the radio while I was making breakfast. It's one of my favourites and I couldn't resist having a little dance around the kitchen.

I was singing away when I noticed Bobby stood in the doorway.

'Hello flower,' I smiled. 'Did my singing disturb you?'

The look on his face was one of horror mixed with fascination.

'This is one of my favourite songs,' I told him. 'Do you like ABBA?'

He shrugged.

'Come and have a little dance before your toast pops up,' I told him.

I took his hands and even though he looked a bit reluctant at first, Bobby was soon jumping up and down to the music.

'I like this song too!' he said.

Soon he was singing along with me.

'I think I've got an ABBA CD in my car,' I told him. 'I'll have to play it for you.'

The following morning on the school run, I put the CD on and I could hear Bobby singing away from the back seat.

'You are the dancing queen, young and sweet only seventeen . . .'

I played it so often after that that he ended up knowing all of the songs off by heart. In my experience, singing was so good for boosting children's self-esteem. It was about encouraging Bobby to use his voice and allowing it to be heard, loud and proud. I loved to hear him singing at the top of his lungs.

All I could do was spend lots of time with Bobby, giving him one-to-one attention. We read books together and played board games like Snakes and Ladders and Cluedo.

There was also something else that I wanted to try.

'I'm going to enrol Bobby in swimming lessons,' I told Patsy when she rang for a catch-up. 'It's something that will keep him active but also help to build up his confidence.'

'I think that's a great idea, Maggie,' she said.

Bobby needed a bit of persuading as he'd never been to a swimming pool before.

'You like the bath, don't you?' I said. 'It's like being in a big bath, you'll love it.'

I was really upbeat and positive about it but it didn't stop him shaking with terror as I led him to the pool on his first lesson.

I watched from the viewing gallery side while Bobby had to be persuaded into the water by the instructor. I'd had a word with her beforehand and she was so patient with him.

At first she got him to sit on the side and dip his feet in the pool. Eventually, much to my relief, she managed to get him into the water. At first, he just splashed up and down the pool while he clung on to the side but it was a start.

'Well done,' I told him afterwards as I got him a packet of crisps from the vending machine. 'You did brilliantly.'

'Are you proud of me?' he asked.

'Of course,' I smiled. 'I'm so proud of you.'

Over the next few weeks he slowly grew in confidence. He was still hesitant in the water but every lesson, Bobby did a little bit more. By the end of the third week, he was using a float and putting his head under the water.

'I was thinking, how would you feel about inviting Daddy to come and watch one of your lessons with me?'

'He wouldn't want to come,' he replied.

'Well we don't know until we ask him,' I said.

Bobby had been doing a weekly session at the contact centre with Dad for the past couple of weeks.

I asked Patsy about Lee coming to Bobby's swimming lesson and she quickly got back to me.

'He said he'd love that,' she told me.

Lee met us at the pool the following week. Bobby's face lit up when he saw him waiting outside the main entrance.

'Oh you came,' he said, sounding surprised.

'Course,' he told him. 'I wanna see you swim, son. I never learnt myself as a kid so I'm happy you're doing it.'

Bobby seemed delighted that Lee was there although he still wanted me to take him into the changing rooms as usual while Lee sat in the viewing area.

When the lesson started, Bobby kept looking over to check that Lee was watching him. This week they were learning to jump into the water. Bobby looked terrified and was last in the queue. When all the other children had jumped in off the side, Bobby hesitated. He looked over at Lee who nodded and gave him a thumbs up.

'You can do it, son,' he shouted.

Bobby reached out for his instructor's hands and launched himself off the side. He closed his eyes as his face hit the water.

'Well done, Bobby,' I clapped. 'You did it.'

I looked over at Lee who, much to my surprise, had tears running down his cheeks. I could see he was embarrassed.

'Sorry,' he mumbled, putting his head down and wiping his eyes on his sleeve. 'I ain't normally a crier. Just seeing Bobby doing stuff like this makes me realise how much he's missed out on. Other kids his age go swimming every weekend but he ain't even been near a pool,' he added. 'He's such a good kid. He deserves better than me.'

'Don't be so hard on yourself,' I told him. 'He doesn't really need swimming lessons. It's love and time with you that he wants. That's what he's really missed out on but you can make that up to him now.'

'I know,' sniffed Lee. 'I just feel so guilty for what I put him through.'

'You were a victim too,' I told him.

They both had so much healing to do.

When Bobby came out of his lesson, he was buzzing with excitement.

'Did you see me, Dad?' he asked Lee. 'I jumped in all by myself.'

'I did,' he nodded. 'You did really good, son.'

'Daddy was so proud,' I told Bobby.

'Shall we get you a packet of salt and vinegar crisps to celebrate?' Lee told him. 'A little bird told me you like crisps.'

'Yay!' cheered Bobby.

As the pair of them walked over to the vending machine in reception, I saw Bobby reach for Lee's hand. It was just a little gesture but it left a lump in my throat. It meant so much to see him skip along next to his dad. In just a few weeks, Bobby had come so far and their connection was really developing.

Another thing children who have been abused or neglected find difficult is expressing their opinion. Bobby had never been asked what he wanted so he'd learnt that his opinion didn't matter and wasn't valid. Even asking him a simple question like what he fancied for tea would send him into a spiral of confusion.

'I don't know,' he replied one night.

I knew he found it very difficult.

'Shall we make some pasta?' I asked and he shrugged.

'What about fish cakes? Or a shepherd's pie?'

Bobby just couldn't make a decision.

'Let's have shepherd's pie,' I told him. 'And you can help me cook it.'

I showed him, under strict supervision, how to chop the onions and carrots. Then we softened them in a pan and browned the mince.

'That's it,' I told him, as he stirred it round with a wooden spoon. 'You're doing such a good job.'

I tipped it all into a baking dish and then we smoothed mashed potato over the top. I'd saved a bit so Bobby could put it into a piping bag and I watched as he piped a smiley face in mash on the top.

'Lovely,' I told him. 'It's smiley pie for tea.'

Bobby giggled.

When we took it out of the oven forty minutes later, Bobby's smiley face had gone all crispy and crunchy.

'That looks absolutely delicious,' I said. 'You are a brilliant chef. Will you cook dinner for us every night?'

All of these little day-to-day things helped to build up his confidence and made him feel good about himself. It had a knock-on effect at school too.

At pick-up one day, Miss Rose, Bobby's class teacher, pulled me to one side.

'Bobby's doing so well at the moment,' she said. 'He's started putting his hand up to answer questions and he's more confident about speaking in front of the rest of the class. He's always been so quiet.'

It was wonderful to hear.

She said she was thinking about making him a library monitor.

'I wanted to speak to you first to see if you thought it was a good idea.'

'Absolutely,' I said. 'I think Bobby would love that.'

I knew he'd come home from school really chuffed one afternoon because Miss Rose had picked him to take the register to the office.

A couple of nights later, he came home from school, beaming.

'Guess what?' he said. 'Miss Rose said I can be a library monitor.'

'That's amazing,' I told him. 'What does the library monitor do?'

'I collect all of the books and put them back on the shelves,' he explained. 'Then when a kid wants a book, I tell them where to find it. I know where all the books are now, Maggie, so I can show people.'

'That's fantastic,' I said.

I could see how proud he was.

However, a week later, he looked downcast when I picked him up from school. He'd been quiet for the past couple of days but today he looked close to tears.

'What is it, Bobby?' I asked him on the way home.

'Can you speak to Miss Rose and tell her I don't want to be the library monitor no more,' he told me.

'But why not?' I asked. 'I thought you really wanted to do it.'

'No, it's stupid,' he blurted.

I was confused about what had changed his mind as he had seemed to be relishing the responsibility. A phone call from Miss Rose later that afternoon when we got home answered my question.

'I wanted to give you a call about Bobby,' she told me. 'One of my colleagues found him crying in the library this lunchtime.'

'Oh no,' I sighed. 'What happened? He mentioned when I picked him up that he didn't want to be a monitor any more.'

'I'm afraid it's come to light that another child has been bullying him,' she said. 'Unbeknown to the staff, they've been coming into the library with their friends and calling him names and today they've admitted to pushing him.'

I was horrified.

'The head is dealing with them and I can assure you there will be repercussions,' she told me.

I was gutted as Bobby had been growing in confidence every day.

'Can you tell me who the child was?' I asked.

'I'm afraid for confidentiality reasons I can't,' said Miss Rose.

'Well, I'm going to ask Bobby about it and I'm sure he will tell me who is responsible,' I said firmly. 'But I'd rather hear it from you first.'

'I understand,' she sighed. 'It's such a difficult situation for everybody.'

She paused.

'I'm afraid it's Melodie who's been bullying him,' she said. 'Bobby's sister.'

SIXTEEN

Moving Forwards

I was absolutely furious. It was impossible for poor Bobby to escape his past, even at school.

When I came off the phone, I went to chat to him about it. He was curled up on the sofa watching TV so I went and sat beside him.

'Miss Rose just called me,' I told him. 'What happened in the library at school today, lovey?'

I wanted Bobby to tell me in his own words what had gone on.

'Nothing,' he mumbled.

'Well, Miss said you were really upset and in tears about it so something must have happened.'

'Melodie was mean to me but there's no point telling anybody cos everyone always believes her.'

His voice was quiet and he wouldn't look at me.

I put my hand on his.

'Bobby, I will always believe you when you tell me something,' I told him. 'That might not have happened when you lived with Brianna but you've got to understand and trust that people believe you now.

'If people didn't believe what you were saying then Brianna wouldn't be in trouble with the police. I believe you, your dad believes you, Patsy believes you and so do your teachers, OK?'

He nodded.

'Now tell me what Melodie did.'

He took a deep breath and cleared his throat.

'She came into the library and she wasn't being kind,' he told me. 'She said I was stupid and useless and I was smelly. Then she threw some books on the floor and tripped me up and all her friends laughed.'

'I'm so sorry to hear that, Bobby. Has she done that before?'

He nodded.

'Every lunchtime since I was library monitor,' he said. 'She was sneaky though. She always did it so Miss didn't see her.'

'I'm sorry, Bobby,' I told him. 'She's going to have to talk to the head teacher because you're right, that isn't kind behaviour and she can't treat you like that.'

I explained that Melodie was going to be punished but that he needed to keep talking to me.

'If things like this happen at school then you need to tell me,' I urged him. 'I can help you to sort it out. Miss Rose said she's going to make sure that Melodie doesn't cause you any other problems but, if she does, then you need to tell us.

'And I don't think you should give up being a library monitor just because of her, do you?'

Bobby shook his head.

'Good lad,' I told him.

★

The next day when Bobby was at school, I rang Patsy and told her what had happened.

'Poor kid,' she sighed. 'Melodie really gives him a rough ride. Maggie, do you want me to talk to Sue and Derek about it? I could set up a meeting with us all?'

'No,' I replied. 'I've talked to Bobby and I know he's OK so I think the best thing to do is to let the school deal with it. It's happened on school time so they will decide what happens to Melodie.'

Melodie was in Year Six – her final year in primary school – so the most they would do was take away her play times and any other privileges.

'OK,' Patsy replied. 'But if she bothers Bobby again then I think we need to get Sue involved. I do know that she's been finding her very difficult.'

Something else was on my mind.

'Do you think that ultimately Bobby needs to change schools?' I asked her. 'We could transfer him to one nearer here?'

It was the only way to really distance him from Melodie and to truly have a fresh start.

'I think we need to wait and see what happens,' Patsy told me. 'Everything is still very up in the air.'

I knew that she was right. We needed to see what the outcome of Brianna's court case was and that would clarify where Melodie and Poppy would live. We also needed to know what was going to happen with Lee and Bobby.

'Also, whatever happens, Melodie is only going to be at

that school until July then she'll be going to secondary school,' added Patsy.

'That's true,' I agreed.

However, it was only February and July seemed like a long way away when Bobby was facing bumping into Melodie at school every day.

That afternoon, Miss Rose pulled me to one side at pick-up.

'Bobby told me that he wants to keep on being a library monitor,' she said.

'That's great news,' I nodded. 'We had a little chat about it yesterday.'

She assured me that Melodie had been told that she wasn't allowed to go into the library at break times and could only go in there during lessons with a teacher supervising her.

'Hopefully that will help to make Bobby feel more comfortable,' she said.

That night Sue called me.

'Oh Maggie, I'm so sorry about what happened with Melodie,' she said. 'I'm just ringing to see how Bobby is.'

She explained that Melodie's teacher, Mrs Price, had told her what had gone on in the library.

'It's not your fault,' I told her. 'Bobby's fine. The school seems to have dealt with it so hopefully that will nip it in the bud.'

'Well I've spoken to Melodie about it and I've told her in no uncertain terms to stay away from Bobby.'

I just hoped that, from now on, she did. Bobby needed a clean break and he didn't want or have to have Melodie in his life anymore. I didn't want to risk anyone or anything destroying his confidence and self-esteem at a time when I was doing everything that I could to build it up.

-The following week, it was time for another Looked After Child (LAC) review. Usually, they would only be held every four to six months. However, due to the change in circumstances with the children, Colin, the Independent Reviewing Officer (IRO) had decided to call another one much earlier.

This time it concerned just Bobby and there would be a separate LAC Review at some stage for Melodie and Poppy that I wouldn't be included in. The aim of this review was to see where we were at with Bobby and decide what was going to happen to him moving forward.

Colin still remained as IRO of all three of the children and he was chairing the meeting like last time. There were the usual faces around the meeting table: Patsy; my supervising social worker, Becky; the school deputy head, Mrs Nichols, and Lee.

'Hi Lee,' I smiled. 'I wasn't sure if you'd be coming.'

'If it's about Bobby then there's no way I ain't going to be here,' he said. 'Brianna didn't even say nothing about the last one.'

His face was pretty much healed now. The only sign left of his injuries was a scar on his lip.

'Hello Lee,' said Colin. 'It's good to see you again.'

Colin had met with Lee a couple of days before the meeting to introduce himself and had given him a rundown of what was going to happen.

'Well, reading the files, things have certainly taken a very different trajectory since we last met,' nodded Colin. 'Patsy, can you give us an update on where we're all at?'

'Of course,' she replied. 'There's been a lot happening.'

She talked about how Lee had revealed that it was Brianna

who had been hurting Bobby, which had been backed up by both Lee and Bobby himself.

'Both of them have given a statement to police to corroborate this,' she told us. 'Indeed, as I'm sure Lee will explain himself, he too suffered both physical and mental abuse at Brianna's hands through the course of their relationship.'

'I'm sorry to hear that,' Colin told him.

'Thanks,' Lee nodded, looking embarrassed.

Patsy talked about how the parenting assessment had been paused in light of these new developments.

'Well, let's look at how Bobby's getting on first,' continued Colin.

He turned to Mrs Nichols.

'According to Bobby's class teacher, he's actually been doing really well,' she smiled. 'There have been a few hiccups but generally she's noticed that he's grown a lot in confidence.

'He'll put his hand up occasionally now and speaks in class, which he never would have done before. He doesn't wet himself any more – in fact, that stopped almost as soon as he came into the care system.'

'That all sounds very positive,' agreed Colin.

When it was my turn to address the meeting, I talked about all the things I'd been doing with Bobby to try to boost his self-esteem and self-worth. I also spoke about the fact that we hadn't realised there was an attachment between himself and Poppy.

'We've had a few issues with Melodie but hopefully that has been sorted now,' I said.

Colin was busy scribbling down some notes.

'I suppose what we need to understand now is what is the

thinking about Bobby going forward,' he said. 'I know Lee and I talked about this yesterday. Do you want to tell the meeting your thoughts, Lee?' Colin asked him. 'What would you like to see happen for Bobby?'

Lee drummed his foot on the floor and I could see that he was nervous.

'Bobby's my lad and I want him to live with me,' he said, his voice shaking. 'After everything that's happened, I want to make it up to him.'

'If Lee wants Bobby to live with him full-time, then we'll need to complete the parenting assessment,' nodded Patsy.

Now it would be a single assessment rather than a joint assessment.

'Lee and Brianna had done two weeks of a six-week assessment before these new allegations came to light,' she explained.

'I think we need to continue that then,' agreed Colin. 'And possibly add a few more weeks on if we need to address any concerns. How do you feel Lee is dealing with things after the ordeal that he's been through with Brianna?'

'He's joined a men's group, haven't you, Lee?' she said. 'So he can get some support from others who have also been through domestic abuse and we're hoping to arrange some counselling sessions for him.'

It was hard talking about someone when they were sitting right there but hopefully Lee appreciated that it had to be done.

'Maggie, I understand that you've supervised a few meetings between Lee and Bobby. How do you think they have gone?'

'Initially Bobby was a bit reserved. You'd say that too, wouldn't you, Lee?'

He nodded.

'I think Bobby's still learning to trust his dad,' I continued. 'I think he's still confused and hurt about why Lee didn't protect him when he was with Brianna. But he's slowly getting his head around the fact that his dad was equally as bullied as he was.'

Although it was sometimes awkward talking about these things in front of a parent, Lee wasn't antagonistic. He wanted to make things right and get Bobby back, so these were relevant discussions and he needed to be part of them.

Colin was also keen to get some joint assessments done of Bobby and Lee together.

'Yes, we'd like to do that as part of the parenting assessment,' nodded Patsy.

I also raised the issue of unsupervised contact, which was a possibility now we knew that Lee wasn't a threat to Bobby.

'I think some unsupervised contact outside of the confines of the centre would really benefit both of them,' I said.

'What kinds of things were you thinking of?' asked Colin, peering over his glasses at me.

'Lee could take Bobby swimming or to the cinema?' I suggested. 'I think even something as simple as a trip to the park would be good for both of them.'

'I'd really like that,' nodded Lee.

'We can definitely look at that,' nodded Colin, writing a note.

Colin also wanted to talk about housing.

'Lee told me that he's currently living in a hostel,' said Colin. 'Clearly that's not going to be a long-term option if he is hoping to have Bobby back with him full-time.'

'That ain't forever,' Lee chipped in. 'I wanna get my own flat. I wouldn't take any kid of mine to live in that hostel.'

Patsy confirmed that they were hoping to get Lee on the housing list for a two-bedroom flat.

'I suppose the one thing we do need to clarify is whether Lee is going to face criminal charges, as that could change everything,' said Colin. 'We need to ascertain that before we even think about moving forwards.'

'Well actually I do have some news about that if Lee doesn't mind me sharing it with you,' said Patsy.

'Yeah,' he said. 'A copper called me this morning.'

Patsy told us that she'd got an email that morning from DC Fleming.

'The police have confirmed that they won't be pressing any charges for failure to act against Brianna.'

I smiled at Lee.

'That must be such a relief for you,' I told him.

'It is,' he sighed. 'It's massive. I feel like a weight's been lifted.'

He looked like he was close to tears.

'I thought I might go to prison,' he admitted. 'To be honest, part of me feels like I would have deserved it. I can't believe I let her do that to my son. I deserve to be punished; nothing can ever make that up to him.'

'Lee, I think you've been punished enough,' I told him.

'I can't believe I didn't stop her,' he told Colin. 'I'll never, ever forgive myself for that. But I swear to you, I'm gonna make it up to him. I'm gonna do everything I can to be a good dad.'

'I can see that, Lee,' nodded Colin. 'At least the worst is over now.'

'But it ain't over yet,' shrugged Lee. 'I still don't know whether Brianna is gonna admit it or not.'

'Yes, we're still waiting to hear when Brianna's plea hearing is going to be,' added Patsy.

I knew all of us were hoping that she would admit everything and plead guilty to all charges. Otherwise, Lee would have to give evidence and there was a chance Bobby would too, depending on whether or not his recorded statements were deemed to be enough.

As Colin wrapped the meeting up, I felt pleased. It had been a really positive meeting – things were finally moving forward and a possible plan was coming together for Bobby.

I had a chat with Patsy afterwards.

'What are the plans for the girls?' I asked her.

'We don't know yet,' she told me. 'We're waiting to hear the outcome of Brianna's case.'

She said that things were going better with their biological dad, Mike.

'It's going to take time for them to establish a relationship but it's going well so far,' she said. 'So we've got that in mind as a possible long-term option. Mike and his new partner don't have any children but they've said they are willing to look at possibly taking the girls on.'

'That's really positive news,' I said.

Things were finally moving on at last for the children and slowly plans were coming together for them.

It was also important to get Bobby on board with what was happening. Nobody had actually asked him yet whether he wanted to live with Lee full-time so Patsy needed to talk to him about it. She popped round the following afternoon after school.

We were playing Snakes and Ladders at the kitchen table when she arrived.

'Ooh, can I have a game?' Patsy asked.

Bobby looked at me.

'Well I think Bobby will be up for it but be careful, Patsy,' I joked, 'he's very good at it and he might beat you.'

'I bet I will,' he told her shyly. 'I always beat Maggie.'

'I have heard that!' she laughed.

After Bobby had thrashed her at a couple of games and I'd got us all a drink, she had a chat with him.

'Bobby, we've been talking a lot to Daddy about how he's feeling and what he wants in the future,' she explained. 'He's told us that he'd love to get a flat with two bedrooms. And Daddy was also telling us how much he would like it if you could go and live with him there. How would you feel about that, Bobby?'

Bobby's face wrinkled with confusion. He fiddled with the counters on the Snakes and Ladders board.

'Will I still see Maggie?' he asked eventually.

'Of course you will,' I told him. 'Even if you live with Daddy, I'll always be here so you can come and visit me whenever you want, flower.'

Bobby nodded.

'I know a good idea!' he said suddenly. 'Why doesn't Daddy move in here with me and Maggie, then he wouldn't need to get no flat?'

Patsy and I looked at each other.

'Bobby, lovey, I'm afraid I don't look after big people,' I told him. 'So we couldn't do that.'

He still looked very unsure.

'Do I have to live with Daddy right now?' he asked.

'Patsy doesn't mean just yet,' I reassured him. 'Daddy needs to show that he's going to look after you and take care of you first, just like he did when you were a baby.'

'We just wanted to see if you liked the idea,' Patsy told him.

'I don't know,' Bobby shrugged.

He looked unsure and it was clear that there was still a lot of work to do for him to truly trust Lee again and feel safe. It wasn't surprising after everything that had happened.

'What are you worried about if you live with Dad?' asked Patsy.

'That Brianna will come back and be mean to us again,' he whispered.

He looked genuinely scared and my heart went out to him.

'Bobby, I promise you that Brianna's not going to come back,' I urged him. 'Daddy wants *you* back, not Brianna.'

I could see that it was going to take more time for him to start truly believing that.

In a bid to help Bobby focus on happier things, we'd been talking lots about his upcoming birthday. He'd decided that he wanted to have a party with a bouncy castle in the local church hall. I didn't want there to be too many people there so we'd decided to invite twelve children from his class.

'Bobby, I want to ask you something,' I told him. 'Would you like Dad to come to your birthday party? He doesn't have to, but if you'd like him to, then I can ask Patsy.'

He thought about it for a while.

'Yes,' he said. 'That might be good.'

I knew I needed to ask Patsy for permission.

'I don't see why not,' she said when I told her. 'I'll see what

Lee thinks but in theory, yes. You'll be there and I think it's very positive that Bobby wants his dad there as well.'

'Great,' I said.

When Patsy called back later that afternoon, I assumed she was ringing about the party.

'Maggie,' she said. 'I need to speak to you.'

My heart sank when I heard the tone of her voice and I instantly knew it wasn't about the party.

'What is it?' I asked. 'What's happened?'

'I've just had a call from DC Fleming,' she said. 'It's Brianna. 'She's pleaded not guilty to all charges.'

Fear crawled up into my throat and lodged itself there.

'Not guilty?' I gasped. 'To what?'

'To all of the charges,' replied Patsy. 'Both ABH and child cruelty.'

The one thing we were all dreading had come true. It would mean there would be a trial. Both Lee and Bobby could be called to court to give evidence – not what either of them needed. This was just the beginning, not the end as I had hoped.

SEVENTEEN

Learning to Live

I looked around the kitchen and smiled. Everything was ready and it looked perfect.

It was Bobby's birthday the following day. There was a little pile of presents on the table and I'd tied a number 9 balloon on to one of the chairs.

Any hopes I had for a sleep-in were dashed when I heard footsteps padding into my room at six-thirty the following morning.

'Good morning, birthday boy,' I smiled.

It was still dark as we padded downstairs. Bobby pushed open the kitchen door and his face lit up when he saw the gifts.

'Are those for me?' he gasped.

'Yes,' I smiled. 'All for you to keep, to wish you happy birthday.'

I'd bought him some more LEGO sets and a couple more board games that I thought he'd enjoy playing. I hadn't gone overboard as I didn't want it to be too overwhelming for him.

Most children would have had the paper ripped off in seconds but Bobby hung back.

'Do you want me to help you open them?' I asked him.

'No,' he said, shaking his head. 'Are you sure they're for me?'

'Does anyone else in this house have a birthday today?' I asked and he shook his head. 'Well I think we can safely say that they're for you then.'

Slowly he picked up each gift and gave it a good feel and tried to guess what it was.

'I think this is a book,' he said. 'Or maybe some chocolate?'

I shook my head.

'A jigsaw?'

'Why don't you open it and see,' I laughed.

Very carefully and cautiously he tore off the wrapping paper.

Bless him, I thought, as I realised his little hands were shaking with excitement.

'I ain't never opened no birthday presents before,' he grinned.

He beamed when he saw the Labyrinth game.

'I thought you and Daddy could play it together,' I suggested.

'Or you and me?' he replied.

It was Bobby's party that afternoon and Lee had arranged to meet us at the church hall at lunchtime to help me set up.

'I've already got Louisa coming to give me a hand so you don't have to,' I'd told him.

'No, I want to,' he replied.

He'd asked me who Louisa was and I'd explained that it was her flat that I had been at the day he'd been following me and I'd confronted him in the street. He sounded mortified.

'I'm sorry,' he'd told me. 'I'll always regret that. I didn't mean to scare you.'

'It's OK,' I'd replied. 'I didn't have any idea what you were going through with Brianna at the time.'

That morning, Bobby was full of questions about his party. He wanted to know who was coming, when it was going to start and finish and what they were going to do at it.

I could see he was getting a bit anxious about it so I talked him through it.

'It's going to be really fun,' I told him. 'It's a chance to have fun with your friends from school and eat lots of treaty food. And your friends might bring you presents.'

'More presents?' he asked, his eyes as wide as saucers. 'I think I like presents.'

'Me too,' I laughed.

I spent the rest of the morning prepping for the party. I'd made each of the kids a lunchbox with a cheese sandwich, a little packet of crisps and an apple. I'd even put some carrot and cucumber sticks in there although I knew in all likelihood they weren't going to eat them! Once everything was ready, I loaded it into the car and Bobby and I headed to the church hall.

'Look who's here,' I said as we pulled up in the car park.

Lee was waiting there outside the entrance. He waved when he saw Bobby.

'Happy birthday, son,' he smiled.

He handed him a present and a card.

'Is that for me?' he asked and Lee nodded.

'It's not much,' he told him. 'Just something I got from the charity shop. I hope you like it.'

'Look, Maggie,' beamed Bobby. 'I got another one.'

'I told you birthdays were good,' I laughed again.

Bobby carefully unwrapped it to find a little plastic travel chessboard.

'It's a game,' Lee told him. 'I don't know how to play but I thought we could learn together.'

Bobby nodded. 'I've seen one of them at school.'

Lee helped me to pin up some balloons on the walls and some 'Happy Birthday' banners. Bobby watched, fascinated.

'I ain't had a birthday before have I, Dad?' he said. 'But I think I like them.'

Lee looked mortified.

'Bri wouldn't let me give him a birthday,' he confessed. 'The poor lad did nothing, though when he was little we used to have a little birthday tea at the flat with my mum,' Lee smiled sadly. 'He used to love it. He probably won't remember as he was only young. Then Mum died and Brianna wouldn't let him do anything. She wouldn't even let me mention to him that it was his birthday.'

'You did the best you could,' I told him. 'You've both been through a lot.'

Soon the company came to set up the bouncy castle and it was time for Bobby's friends to start arriving.

I hope I've done the right thing, having a party, I thought to myself.

But I really wanted Bobby to have the opportunity to feel special and celebrate his birthday for the first time, that he remembered. Thankfully he seemed fine as he threw himself around on the bouncy castle with some other children from his class.

'He looks like he's having a great time,' smiled Louisa as she stood holding Edie in her arms.

'I'm so pleased. He said he wanted a party but I wasn't sure that I'd done the right thing.'

A dozen friends didn't seem too many and they all screamed and giggled as they jumped around on the bouncy castle, their cheeks flushed and their hair plastered with sweat. While they all settled down to eat their lunchboxes, Louisa helped me to sort out the cake. As a surprise, I'd got my friend Vicky to make Bobby a Snakes and Ladders cake and I put nine candles into it. His name was spelt out on the board in blue letters.

'Wow, Vicky's done a brilliant job,' said Louisa as she got out some matches.

Vicky was a fellow foster carer but she was also a talented baker and she really enjoyed doing it. I didn't know where she found the time.

Louisa lit all the candles and slowly and carefully, I carried the cake from the kitchen and into the main hall.

I started off the singing.

'Happy birthday to you . . . happy birthday dear Bobby, happy birthday to you.'

Everybody clapped and cheered. But as I put the cake down in front of Bobby, the look on his face was one of pure panic.

He stared at it.

'Go on, Bobby,' his friend shouted.

Everyone was waiting, looking at him expectantly, waiting for him to blow out the candles.

Suddenly Bobby pushed back his chair, stood up and ran out of the hall. I panicked and looked at Louisa.

'You go after him,' she told me. 'I'll deal with this.'

She blew out the candles while I ran outside to find Bobby. I didn't have far to go. He was sat outside, crying. Lee came running out behind me.

'Son, what's wrong?' he asked.

Bobby looked up.

'What's he doing here?' he sobbed to me. 'I want him to go away. I don't want him here.'

I looked at Lee.

'I'm sorry, Lee – let me have a quick chat with Bobby then we'll come back in.'

Lee looked devastated and he went back inside the hall, dejected.

I sat down next to Bobby on the cold, hard ground.

'What happened in there?' I asked. 'Did you not like your cake?'

'Everyone was looking at me and shouting and I didn't know what to do,' he said.

He started to cry.

'I don't know how to do birthdays.'

'Oh lovey,' I sighed. 'When you have a cake and it's your birthday, you're supposed to blow out the candles.'

He looked at me blankly.

'Didn't you realise that?'

He shook his head.

'I wasn't allowed no birthday and I had to stay in my room when the girls had their one.'

'You must have been to someone else's birthday party?' I asked.

'Brianna didn't let me. I got a piece of paper lots of times to go to a party but she crumpled them up and threw them in the bin.'

'I'm so sorry, flower. I didn't realise you didn't know what to do.'

Maybe I had been wrong to suggest a party to him. I managed to persuade him to go back inside for the last ten minutes.

Thankfully Louisa had got everyone organised with a piece of cake and the kids were now all back on the bouncy castle again.

'Is Bobby OK?' Lee asked me, looking concerned.

I nodded.

'I'll explain later,' I told him.

The rest of the party went OK, although I could see Bobby was exhausted.

'Why don't I take Bobby and Edie back to the flat to give you time to clear up?' Louisa suggested when the last child had been collected.

'Good idea,' I told her.

'I can stay and help you,' offered Lee.

He cleared all the leftover food into bin bags while I swept the floor.

'What was wrong with Bobby when he got upset before?' he asked me as we popped the balloons.

'The poor thing got overwhelmed by the birthday cake,' I told him. 'Everyone was looking at him and he didn't realise that he had to blow out the candles. He said he'd never done that before or maybe he did know, and he just panicked.'

Much to my surprise, Lee started to cry.

'I've let him down so badly,' he wept. 'How can a kid not know what to do with a birthday cake? It's all my fault. I've damaged him.'

'You've got to forgive yourself and try to move on,' I told him. 'Bobby will be OK.'

Lee shook his head.

'But I've done so much damage to him, he's better off without me. He ain't been a normal kid because of me. He's missed out on so much.'

I tried to reassure him.

'Bobby is starting to understand that you were a victim too,' I told him. 'He knows that Brianna hurt you as well.'

'But he doesn't really want me near him,' he said. 'When he was crying it was you he wanted, not me. He didn't want me to comfort him.'

'It will take time for him to heal,' I reassured him. 'It's not going to be instant. But he will eventually learn to forgive you.'

'I just think maybe what's best for him is for me to walk away,' he sighed. 'I've let him down, I'm weak, and he's better off without me.'

'Is that really what you want?' I asked him firmly. 'Because if it is then it's not fair on Bobby to carry on with the parenting assessment. Do you really want to do that?'

He shook his head.

'Then Bobby needs you to fight for him,' I told him. 'You didn't do that before, but it's time to do it now. This is your chance to fight for him and your relationship and for the right to be his dad.'

I was convinced that what Bobby and Lee needed was some quality time together, just the two of them, so they could build up that trust and get to know each other again.

At the LAC review, it had been agreed that Lee could have the odd session of unsupervised contact so I'd asked Lee if he'd like to take Bobby swimming. I knew there was a family swimming session at the pool where he had his lessons.

I arranged for Lee to take him there one Friday night.

'Remember Dad's going to go swimming with you after school today,' I told Bobby that morning. 'So we must remember to put your swimming stuff in the car.'

'Will you be coming too?' he asked.

'I'll drop you off at the pool,' I told him. 'But I won't come in the water. Daddy will though and he's really looking forward to taking you.'

That afternoon, I picked Bobby up and drove him to the leisure centre where Lee was waiting outside.

'I'm a bit nervous,' he told me as Bobby ran in. 'I can't swim that good and what if he doesn't like it?'

'Just relax and enjoy it,' I said.

'Do you want Dad to take you into the changing rooms?' I asked Bobby.

'Could you help me get changed?' he asked me.

Lee looked disappointed but I didn't want him to get too disheartened.

'Baby steps,' I told him.

I took Bobby into the women's changing rooms and folded his clothes for him while he got into his trunks.

'Have fun with Dad,' I told him.

I let him go out onto the poolside where Lee was waiting.

'See you in an hour,' I said, waving from the changing room entrance. 'Have fun.'

Although I didn't want to show it to Lee, I felt slightly anxious about how it was going to go. Bobby hadn't been on his own with Lee for many months and I hoped that he would be OK. Just to make sure and put my mind at rest, I sat in the viewing area. There were several other people in there so I was hopeful they wouldn't see me.

At first, Bobby was hesitant to even get in the water. He stood on the side of the pool.

'Oh no,' I thought. This was going to end in tears and I was going to have to swoop in. But I knew I had to step back and let Lee deal with it.

Lee stood in the water talking to Bobby. Then he got him to sit down on the side. Eventually he held out his hands to him.

Bobby hesitated.

'Go on Bobs,' I said to myself, willing him to jump in.

Then, very carefully and gently, Lee picked him up and lowered him into the water.

Bobby bounced around in the shallow end for a bit with Lee watching. Then Lee encouraged him to go a bit deeper.

My heart was in my mouth as I saw Bobby stumble, then his head went under the water. I knew he still hated that and would sometimes panic. But, a few seconds later, he emerged laughing.

After ten minutes, much to my relief, the pair were laughing and jumping around together.

I couldn't help but smile as I watched them. It was so lovely to see Lee being playful with his son, free of the added pressure of social workers and contact workers watching their every move.

In fact, it suddenly didn't feel right to be watching them. I felt confident enough now to leave them so I went to the café to get a cup of tea and some cake.

I came back five minutes before the session was due to end. I looked in the pool and Lee was throwing Bobby up into the air and he was laughing. He didn't even object as he went under a few times, something he'd been terrified to do in his lessons.

When the session was up, I was waiting by the entrance to the changing rooms with blue covers over my shoes, holding out Bobby's towel.

'Did you enjoy that, flower?' I asked him and he smiled.

'Yeah it was fun,' he grinned. 'Dad threw me up really high.'

'Can I go in the changing room with Dad?' he asked me.

'I can help him get dressed,' nodded Lee.

'Of course you can,' I said, handing him his towel and rucksack.

As I went to wait for them in reception, I was incredibly moved. It was the first time I'd seen them really bond and it filled me with hope. Maybe this could work out, even after everything that had happened.

Bobby and Lee still saw each other once a week at the contact centre where they would be supervised by a worker. I knew they both found it stressful to be watched and I could see that they were both on edge.

'Could they maybe do an activity together to help them relax into it a bit more?' I suggested to Patsy.

Lee was a lot more natural with Bobby when he felt that he wasn't being judged.

'I'll have a word with Palvi and see if she could suggest something,' she replied.

I knew options were limited in that run-down building.

When I dropped Bobby at the centre a couple of days later, Palvi and Lee were there to meet us.

'Guess what, Bobs?' smiled Lee. 'We're gonna do some cooking.'

Bobby looked at him in amazement.

'What do you mean?' he asked.

'You're going to have tea with Daddy here at the centre but you're going to be cooking it,' Palvi told him.

'But I can't do cooking,' said Bobby.

'I bet you can,' Lee told him. 'Let's give it a go. We're gonna make some pizza.'

'Ooh lovely,' I smiled. 'Make sure you save me some.'

It was lovely to see Bobby's excited little face as he went off with Dad to the kitchen. It was only a run-down little kitchen but that didn't matter.

'They might be slightly longer than the hour today,' Palvi told me.

'That's fine by me,' I told her.

For once, rather than sit in reception, I'd have chance to nip to the supermarket.

When I got back just over an hour later, Bobby came running out to see me.

'Look Maggie, we made pizza,' he shouted. 'And I saved you some.'

He handed me the tiniest slice and I took a nibble.

'Wow! That is delicious!' I gushed.

'You and Dad have done a great job,' smiled Palvi.

Then Lee came wandering out, his T-shirt and jeans all covered in flour.

'Come on, Bobby, we haven't finished – we need to tidy everything up now,' he told him.

'OK Dad,' he sighed. 'Coming.'

He ran back into the kitchen leaving Palvi and I to it.

'It looks like things have gone well,' I said to her.

'Really well,' she said. 'Bobby was a bit quiet at first and he kept asking where you were but he quickly settled into it. And Lee has been the most chatty that I've ever seen him. I think he really enjoyed it.'

I hoped that all of these activities would give them both a chance to develop a lovely, solid bond.

Another activity that I had in mind was the cinema. I ran it by Patsy first and she agreed that it was OK.

'Would you like Daddy to take you to the cinema this weekend?' I asked Bobby one evening.

His face lit up.

'I ain't been there for a long, long time,' he said. 'But I think I can remember it.'

It still surprised me, all of the things that he wasn't allowed to do when he and Lee lived with Brianna.

I suggested it to Lee one night when I picked Bobby up from contact. I thought he would jump at the chance but he looked hesitant.

'Don't you fancy it?' I asked him.

'I do, it's not that,' he said.

He suddenly looked embarrassed.

'I'm just skint,' he admitted. 'I don't think my benefits would stretch to that and then Bobby might want popcorn and I'd hate to say no.'

'Don't worry, I'll pay for it,' I told him. 'I think Bobby would love it and it's another opportunity for you to spend time together, just the two of you.'

MAGGIE HARTLEY

'Thank you,' he said. 'I really appreciate all you're doing for us.'

I knew that every Saturday morning, my local cinema did a kids' screening. This week it was the latest child-friendly film with a couple of cartoons beforehand.

It was within walking distance of my house so that morning, I waved them both off.

'Have fun,' I smiled.

I got on with some cleaning and made some phone calls to my friend Vicky and Louisa. I'd just come off the phone when my mobile rang again. I didn't think anything of it when Lee's number flashed up on the screen.

They're probably on their way back, I thought.

So I was confused when I heard Bobby's panicked voice. He was talking so fast I could hardly understand him.

'Bobby, slow down,' I urged him. 'What is it? What's happened?'

'It's Dad,' he shouted. 'You need to come. He says he's having a heart attack.'

EIGHTEEN

Breaking Point

It was one of those situations where my brain couldn't take in everything I was being told.

'Bobby, where are you?' I asked him, trying to sound calm even though I was anything but.

'We're at the cinema,' he told me. 'Daddy's on the floor. He gave me his phone and pressed the button so I could ring you.'

Panic rose up inside me. What the hell had happened?

'Bobby, is there an adult around?' I asked him. 'Can you give Dad's phone to someone who works there and ask them to help you?'

'Hello,' said a man's voice a few seconds later. He didn't sound very old.

'Can you please tell me what's happened?' I asked.

'The man came out of the cinema, said he couldn't breathe and collapsed,' he said. 'My colleague's called an ambulance. In fact, I can see it pulling up outside now.'

'Please can you make sure you look after the little boy?' I asked him. 'His name is Bobby. He needs to go in the ambulance with his dad . . .'

But he'd already hung up.

I swallowed the lump of anxiety in my throat. I had to trust that they would look after Bobby. They wouldn't just leave a nine-year-old boy on his own, they'd make sure that he went with his dad, wouldn't they?

I knew there was no point driving to the cinema because by the time I got there, the ambulance would already have left. I decided that the best option was to drive to the hospital myself and meet them there. There was only one main hospital in our area that had an A&E, the same one I'd taken Lee to when Brianna had attacked him.

As I grabbed my handbag and got into my car, my head was spinning. What on earth had happened? Lee was in his early thirties and, as far as I knew, there was no reason for him to collapse like that. It must have been so distressing for Bobby to witness it too.

Please God, let him be OK.

I felt sick as I got closer to the hospital, not knowing what kind of situation I was about to face. It took me ages to find a parking spot but eventually I got sorted and ran into A&E.

'I'm looking for the man who came in by ambulance from the Odeon cinema,' I told the woman behind the Perspex screen as I gave her Lee's details. 'He would have had a little boy with him . . .'

I was interrupted by a someone calling my name.

'Maggie! Maggie!' said a familiar voice.

I swung round to see Bobby sitting on a plastic chair in

the corner. He was next to a man who looked like he was wearing a paramedic's uniform.

'Oh lovey,' I sighed, running over and putting my arms around him. 'Are you all right?'

He nodded.

'What happened to Daddy?'

'We watched a bit of the film then he started making funny noises,' he said shakily, his eyes wide with fear. 'He said he couldn't breathe and he didn't feel well and we had to go outside. Then he fell down on the floor.'

'You poor thing,' I soothed. 'That must have been so scary for you. But don't worry, Dad's safe now and the doctors are looking after him.'

Bobby nodded but understandably I could see that he was shaken up.

The paramedic, a young lad in his twenties, introduced himself as Jake.

'Do you know where Lee is?' I asked him.

'The gentleman's been taken through there,' he told me. 'The doctors are with him now.'

'Do you know what's wrong with him?"

'I don't know anything else at the moment, I'm afraid,' he said. 'One of my colleagues asked me to sit with the young lad as he got called to another job.'

'I understand,' I told him. 'Would you be OK to wait with Bobby for a little while longer while I nip through and see how Lee is?'

'Sure, I can do that,' he replied.

'Thank you,' I nodded.

I made sure I told Bobby what was happening.

'I'm just going to go and have a word with the doctors,' I said.

He looked panicked.

'I'm coming back, I promise,' I reassured him. 'I want to check that Daddy's OK. You wait here with Jake for a few minutes.'

Bobby looked close to tears as I walked off.

I wandered aimlessly down the corridor looking into all the bays, hoping for a glimpse of Lee.

'Can I help you?' a nurse asked me eventually.

'I'm looking for Lee,' I told her. 'I think he's just been brought in from the Odeon cinema.'

I explained who I was and showed her my carer's ID.

'I'm currently fostering his son who was with him when he collapsed.'

She went to the board to check.

'Come with me,' she said, leading me to a cubicle.

When she pulled the curtain back, there was Lee. He was lying on a trolley with an oxygen mask over his face. He looked ashen.

'Lee,' I gasped. 'What on earth happened?'

He fumbled to take the mask off.

'No, no, don't take that off,' I gasped.

'It's OK,' he croaked. 'I'm much better now.'

He explained that he'd started to feel funny shortly after the film started.

'Everything was spinning. I couldn't breathe, then my chest felt tight, my heart was racing then I got these horrible pains down my arms.

'I thought I was having a heart attack,' he said. 'I told Bobby we needed to leave. Poor lad looked terrified, then we came out and I just went down. I honestly thought I was a goner.'

I was about to ask what the doctors had said when suddenly the curtain was pulled back and one walked in.

'Good news,' he told Lee. 'Your ECG was normal and all of your vitals are in the normal range so you're free to go.'

'But what do you think might have made him feel like that and make him collapse?' I asked, confused.

'I think it's more than likely you were having a panic attack,' said the doctor. 'I've done some bloods as well just to make sure, but I suspect they will also come back as normal.'

'I feel bloody stupid,' sighed Lee. 'I swear I was having a heart attack. I could feel the pain in my chest.'

'I can assure you that your heart looks fine,' the doctor told him.

'I'll just give you a couple of other quick checks, just to reassure you.'

I stepped outside the cubicle to give him a bit of privacy. Five minutes later, the doctor pulled back the curtain.

'How's he doing?' I asked.

'His pulse is normal, his temperature is normal, he's breathing easily now,' he said. 'I've told Lee that I think the best course of action is to refer him to a psychiatrist.'

Lee's face fell.

'Psychiatrist?' he gasped. 'I ain't a nutter.'

'No one said you are, Lee,' I told him. 'You've just come out of an extremely traumatic relationship where you were mentally and physically abused. It's no surprise your mental health has suffered. Your body has probably just started to process that trauma.'

The doctor eventually left us to it.

'What really happened at the cinema, Lee?' I asked him. 'Did something trigger it?' I knew enough about panic attacks to know that they sometimes had a trigger.

Lee looked away.

'I thought I saw her,' he muttered. 'In the cinema.'

'Brianna?'

Lee nodded.

He described how, just as the lights had gone down, he'd seen a woman with bleached blonde hair sitting a few rows in front of them.

'I could only see the back of her head but I was sure it was her,' he said. 'She was even with a kid Poppy's age. Sitting there in the dark, it brought it all back. Even just seeing her made me feel so scared.'

His eyes filled with tears.

'It's weird, it's like my body was back there again. The hairs on the back of my neck stood up and I went all shaky. It was horrible, Maggie. My heart was racing, my head was spinning. I couldn't stay in there no more.'

'Do you think it was her?' I asked.

'I doubt it,' he shrugged. 'She lives over the other side of town and she didn't normally take the girls down the cinema. But by then, I'd talked myself into thinking it was her.'

A tear rolled down his cheek.

'I feel so pathetic,' he whispered. 'How can I be so scared of a grown woman?'

'I'm not surprised, Lee,' I told him, putting my hand on his shoulder. 'You and Bobby have been through so much.

'I think the doctor's right,' I added. 'You need to see a professional and talk it all through.'

Then I asked him if it had happened before and he nodded.

'Different things set me off,' he said. 'Once it was hearing a song that was playing on the radio one time when she was battering me. Another time it was when I smashed a glass in my room at the hostel and the noise sent me into a panic. It's stupid really.'

He also described how he'd been having regular nightmares and flashbacks.

'Lee, you should have said something sooner,' I told him. 'You should have mentioned this to Patsy.'

'I felt stupid,' he replied. 'I didn't want to look weak.'

'You've been through so much, it's to be expected,' I reassured him. 'Sometimes it helps to talk things through with somebody.'

But Lee just looked exhausted and his face was etched with worry.

'Are you going to tell Patsy what happened?' he asked me.

'I've got to,' I said. 'I don't want to call her on a Saturday but I'll put it in my recordings and I'm sure she'll want to have a chat to you about it.'

She wasn't Lee's social worker, she was Bobby's, so I wasn't under any obligation to report it to her, but I knew that she'd want to know what had happened.

'Let's get you home,' I told him. 'Bobby and I will drop you back at the hostel.'

'Thanks,' he said.

I could tell he was still a bit wobbly so I helped him to put his coat on and manoeuvre himself off the trolley.

We walked slowly back to reception where Bobby was still with the paramedic.

'Dad!' he said, jumping up and running towards him. 'You're OK!'

'I'm fine, son. It was just my stupid mind playing tricks on me.'

Bobby still looked worried.

'What happened then?' he asked. 'What happened with your heart?'

'Daddy's heart is absolutely fine,' I told him. 'There's no need to worry. He's going to be OK.'

'Come on,' I said, ruffling Bobby's hair. 'Let's go and drop your dad off at his place and then we can go home.'

The hostel where Lee was living was a brick building at the end of a residential street. A couple of the windows were broken and boarded up and there was a group of men sitting on the floor outside swigging from cans of lager.

'I'd invite you in but it's no place for a kiddie,' sighed Lee.

'It's OK,' I told him. 'You must be shattered after everything that happened today.

'Look after yourself, Lee.'

'Bye bye, Dad,' waved Bobby.

'I'll see you soon, son,' he replied.

Now we were on our own, I was finally able to check that Bobby was OK.

'How are you doing, flower?' I asked him. 'That must have been really scary for you today.'

'Yeah it was, but the cinema people called an ambulance and the ambulance people said I was really brave.'

'Well, you were,' I said. 'You did ever so well to call me. I bet your daddy is very proud of you.

'He's going to be OK you know,' I added, reassuring him again. 'He's going to talk to someone about how he's feeling and they will hopefully be able to help him.'

'Has he got a poorly head?' asked Bobby.

'Yes he has,' I smiled. 'That's a really good way of putting it.'

I knew that Lee, and perhaps Bobby too, were going to need ongoing support in order to keep moving forwards.

On Monday, Patsy gave me a call.

'I've just read your notes from the weekend,' she said. 'How's Lee?'

'He's actually doing OK,' I told her. 'The doctors checked him over but they said that he's fine.'

'What on earth happened?'

I shrugged.

'The doctor seemed to think that it was psychological rather than physical,' I said. 'It sounds like he was having a panic attack.'

I explained what Lee had told me, about thinking that he saw Brianna at the cinema.

'He admitted to me that he's been suffering flashbacks and nightmares too,' I said.

'Poor guy,' she sighed. 'I'll have a chat to my manager and see if there's any extra support that we can offer him.'

We also discussed the fact that she would put Bobby's name down for some play therapy. I knew that it was often helpful for children who had been through abuse and trauma and it would be a good way for him to process his emotions.

★

Lee still seemed shaken up when I saw him at the contact centre a couple of days later as I dropped Bobby off. He looked pale and there were dark shadows under his eyes.

'How are you doing?' I asked.

'Not too good,' he replied. 'Since the cinema, the nightmares and the flashbacks are getting worse. It all feels so real. The second I close my eyes, I see her face and I'm back there in the flat.'

It had made Lee realise that he did want the psychiatrist's appointment, although it wasn't for another couple of weeks.

One morning, a few days later, Patsy called me.

'I wanted to update you about Lee's appointment,' she said.

'Oh, has that already happened?' I asked, confused.

Unbeknown to me, Patsy had talked to Lee and she'd managed to move the appointment forward by getting him a cancellation.

She told me that Lee had been diagnosed with something called Complex Post-Traumatic Stress Disorder (CPTSD).

'I've heard of PTSD before, but not that,' I said.

Patsy explained that PTSD related to a single traumatic event but CPTSD was connected to a series of traumatic events over time.

'That would make sense after everything he's been through with Brianna,' I said. 'How can it be treated?'

'There is no treatment as such,' said Patsy. 'Talking therapy can help, and they want Lee to go on antidepressants. He's also going to have some Cognitive Behaviour Therapy, which will give him some coping strategies if he starts to feel himself getting panicked.'

A few days later, I met Lee in the park with Bobby.

'I'm pleased that you had your appointment,' I told him. 'Patsy said they gave you some suggestions about what might help.'

'Yeah, I've just been to pick up my medication from the chemist,' he replied.

However, as we watched Bobby play on the playground, he seemed very downcast.

'What is it, Lee?' I asked. 'Are you still struggling to sleep?'

'I'm just worried,' he sighed. 'What if all of this is held against me and I'm not allowed to get Bobby back? What if Social Services think if I'm seeing a psychiatrist and I'm on tablets then I'm not a good dad.'

'Lee, they won't think that,' I reassured him.

I explained that many parents that Social Services dealt with were on antidepressants, or were having counselling or therapy.

'It's honestly not a problem,' I told him. 'To be honest, it's to be expected after everything that you've been through. If you do have issues with your mental health, it's how you're addressing them and dealing with them that counts. The fact that you're seeking help, taking medication and talking about things will be seen as a positive.'

No one was going to hold it against Lee if he was trying to work through the horrendous trauma that he had suffered.

'I won't fail the parenting assessment because of that?' he asked again.

'No,' I replied. 'It just shows that you're trying to be the best father you can to Bobby.'

I knew Lee needed all the help he could get and I so wanted his mental health to be in a good place. Over the next few weeks, I knew he was going to be facing some of his biggest challenges. He was approaching the end of his parenting assessment but it was also the beginning of Brianna's trial. More than ever, Lee needed to be in a good place for Bobby's sake. Otherwise there was a risk it was all going to come crashing down.

NINETEEN

In the Dock

We all sat around the table at the police station, sipping lukewarm, weak tea out of polystyrene cups. Next to me I could feel Lee jiggling his foot, clearly very nervous.

We were back in the same room that Bobby had been interviewed in all those months ago with the cameras on the walls and the squishy sofa. Today, however, Bobby wasn't with us as he was at school.

'Thanks for coming,' smiled DC Orton. 'Myself and my colleagues just wanted to get together and talk to you about the court proceedings and where things stand at the moment.'

'We would all really appreciate that clarification,' nodded Patsy, getting a pen and paper out of her bag to take notes.

DC Orton was the officer who had first interviewed Bobby about the bruises on his arms. Her colleague, DC Fleming, who had dealt with the ABH charge against Brianna, was also there.

'As you know, Brianna has pleaded not guilty to all the charges against her,' DC Orton explained. 'So unfortunately that means that there's going to be a trial.'

They had been liaising with the Crown Prosecution Service about how that was going to be done.

'Will Brianna be on trial for both charges at the same time?' asked Patsy.

It was exactly what I had been wondering for the past few weeks too.

'Because they're two very different charges – one being against an adult and the other concerning a child – the courts want to deal with them separately,' DC Fleming chipped in.

'But it's important to note that if Brianna is found guilty of both and gets a custodial sentence, which is likely, those sentences will run consecutively, not concurrently.'

It was all so complicated and confusing. My main concern was the child cruelty charges. I knew there was a good chance that Bobby would be called to give evidence at that trial. I knew that was on Lee's mind too in relation to the ABH court case.

'I got a letter to say there's a court case scheduled for two weeks' time,' said Patsy. 'So which of the charges does that relate to?'

'Brianna will be on trial for ABH against Lee first,' DC Fleming told us. 'The child cruelty case will be dealt with at a later date once the first trial has concluded.'

I breathed a sigh of relief. Although the verdict concerned Bobby, he was unlikely to be called as a witness. Poor Lee looked absolutely terrified.

'Don't worry, Lee, the Crown Prosecution Service will explain it all and go through it with you,' Patsy told him.

DC Fleming nodded.

'We can arrange a meeting for you next week with the prosecution barrister and they can talk you through everything,' he said. 'They can even organise for you to have a tour of the Crown Court if it would help you to feel more comfortable and confident.'

Lee nodded, but I could see that he was already worrying about it.

'Lee, you're going to be called as a prosecution witness,' DC Fleming explained. 'But because of the nature of the charges, I can assure you that you won't have to face Brianna in court.'

He explained that he could give evidence from behind a screen.

'So Brianna will be able to hear you but not see you and she won't be in your view,' he added.

Lee shook his head.

'I don't want no screen,' he said confidently. 'I want to see her. I want to prove to myself and to her that she can't hurt me any more.'

'Are you sure that's a good idea, Lee?' Patsy asked him but he seemed determined.

'It'll be horrible but I want to look her in the eye. I want her to know that she doesn't have any power or control over me any more.'

It was a brave move but I worried about the effect it would have on Lee. He'd had a rocky few weeks with his mental health and had been noticeably struggling since collapsing at the cinema.

'When do you think she might be on trial for the child cruelty charges?' I asked. 'I'd like to start preparing Bobby for the fact he might have to give evidence.'

'Absolutely,' nodded DC Orton. 'As you know I'm sure, to help children feel comfortable, they're able to have a tour of the courtroom and talk everything through with the prosecution barrister and ask any questions. He would definitely be able to give his evidence from behind a screen or ideally via video link from another room in the court.'

'I think video link would be the best option,' I nodded.

It was only a short meeting but at least we were all aware of what there was to come.

'It's really going to drag on over the next few months,' said Patsy. 'I'll also have to have a chat with Sue as potentially Melodie and Poppy could be called as witnesses for either trial.'

Even though the courts did what they could, it was still an ordeal for any child having to give evidence in legal proceedings. Even just stepping inside a court as an observer gave me nervous flutters in my stomach.

After the meeting, Patsy, Lee and I had a little debrief in the car park.

'At least now we know what's happening,' Patsy sighed.

'Do you think I should tell Bobby what's going on?' I asked.

'I don't think so,' she replied. 'I think he'll only worry if he knows Lee has got to go to court. His court case might be months off yet so I think we only speak to him about it when we know that it's imminent.'

'I agree,' nodded Lee. 'I don't want him worrying. That bi**h has already put us both through enough.'

I could see that Lee was really agitated at the thought of having to give evidence.

'What if I can't do it?' he frowned. 'What if I have one of them panics and collapse? I ain't seen Brianna since that day she beat me up.'

I could see that he was in mental turmoil.

'Lee, I'll be there to support you' Patsy told him. 'Everyone is on your side.'

'What about you, Maggie?' he asked. 'Will you come too?'

'Of course,' I smiled. 'You've got my support if you want it.'

At the beginning of all this, I'd got the wrong impression of Lee entirely. As time had gone on and I'd seen him around Bobby, I could tell that he genuinely loved his son and was desperate to make things up to him.

Patsy pointed out to Lee that none of us would actually be able to be with him as he wouldn't be allowed to sit in court through the trial as he was a witness.

'You can't be in court until after you've given evidence,' she said. 'The prosecutor will explain it to you but you'll have to wait in a room until you're called by the court staff.'

I could see Lee's head was spinning as he tried to take in all the information. He looked so worried.

'It's going to be OK,' I told him. 'If Bobby can do it then you can too. It will all be over soon.'

However, I fully understood why the thought of facing Brianna in court was terrifying for him. When Lee had left, I had a quick word with Patsy.

'I worry about the effect this court case is going to have on his mental health,' I said. 'He's already very fragile and he's only into the first few weeks of his talking therapy.'

'He'll be OK,' reassured Patsy. 'In a way it might provide some sort of closure for him being able to face Brianna in court.'

I wasn't so sure.

'As long as he gets the right outcome,' I said.

★

As Brianna's trial edged ever closer, I hardly slept. I was worrying about everything – Lee, Bobby, the court case, the parenting assessment, what was going to happen. So many worst-case scenarios ran through my mind – what if Lee didn't turn up to give evidence? What if he had a panic attack? What if Brianna was found not guilty?

On the morning the trial was due to start, I felt quite deceitful as I got ready for court, as Bobby wasn't aware any of this was happening.

'Oh you look posh, Maggie,' he smiled, as I came downstairs after breakfast.

I'd swapped my usual jeans and jumper for a blue shirt and black trousers. I was driving to the court straight after the school run and even though I wasn't directly involved with proceedings, I liked to look smart.

I felt guilty that I hadn't told him where I was going and the fact that Brianna was on trial for hurting his dad.

'Thank you,' I told him. 'I've got an appointment this morning.'

Thankfully he didn't ask what it was.

'You're not lying to him,' Patsy reassured me as we met up later that morning. 'You're just not telling him the whole truth but it's for his own sake.'

The Crown Court was in a neighbouring town and it was one that I had been to before. It was an old Victorian building and it was very grand and imposing. Patsy was waiting outside the entrance for me.

'Where's Lee?' I asked anxiously. 'Has he not turned up yet?'

'Don't worry, he's here,' she reassured me. 'He needed to be here earlier so he's already gone in.'

I was so relieved that he had turned up.

'How did he seem?' I asked her.

'Very on edge but he seems determined to do it,' she told me. 'He'd even managed to borrow a suit from someone in the hostel so he looked very smart.'

Patsy and I made our way through the main entrance. As with most courts, we had to have our bags checked and we had to walk through a security scanner. We found Brianna's name on the listings and made our way to court number two.

No matter what case it was or why I was there, going to court always made me feel nervous. I think it was just the hushed atmosphere and the air of tension.

Patsy pushed open the heavy door of the court. It was a huge and imposing courtroom with dark wood panelling and an ornate gold crest on the wall behind the raised bench where the judge would sit.

There were a few ushers in there chatting with whom I assumed were the prosecution barristers. The dock was empty, Brianna obviously not in there yet.

Patsy and I made our way to the public gallery where a couple of young women were already seated. I didn't recognise them but guessed they might be friends or family of Brianna's, as they looked a similar age.

Just before 10 a.m., there was a clattering and Brianna was brought into the dock. She was led in by a security guard but as she wasn't on remand, she wasn't handcuffed. It was an open wooden dock, not one of those high-security ones that were enclosed by glass panelling.

I hadn't seen her for several months since those early contact sessions. Her bleached blonde hair had dark roots and she was wearing an ill-fitting grey trouser suit that looked way too big for her. She didn't appear to be distressed or overly worried to be in court. In fact, she smiled and waved at the women in the public gallery.

It was odd to think that this ordinary-looking woman had been capable of such cruelty. She had made Bobby and Lee's lives a misery and I found it hard to look at her without feeling anger rising inside me.

A few minutes later, one of the court clerks led the jury into the jury box. Twelve people filed in and took their seats. They ranged from a man who looked to be in his seventies to a young woman who didn't look much older than a teenager. Some of them looked around nervously, others stared at Brianna in the dock.

Then a hush suddenly descended on the courtroom.

'All rise,' said a loud voice.

Everyone stood up as the judge made his entrance. It was a while since I'd sat in on a court case and I'd forgotten about all of the pomp and ceremony. To me, all judges tended to look the same because of their gowns and wigs. Like today, they were usually well-spoken older men, although I had come across a couple of female judges over the years.

As we sat back down, the judge invited the prosecution barrister to begin his opening statements.

Here goes, I thought.

I wondered how Lee was feeling. I knew it could be a long, tortuous wait for him as he might not even be called to give evidence today. I felt sick at the thought of having to go through it all with Bobby in a few months' time.

But before the prosecutor could begin his opening arguments, I noticed Brianna was waving from the dock.

'What's she doing?' I whispered to Patsy.

'I think she's trying to attract her barrister's attention,' she said.

Finally the defence barrister noticed, stood up and walked over to her in the dock.

Brianna leant over and whispered something in his ear and then he whispered something back.

'Is there a problem, Mr Hughes?' asked the judge snappily, peering over his metal glasses.

The defence barrister walked back to his table.

'Your Honour, could I approach the bench please?' he asked.

Patsy and I looked at each other.

'What's going on?' I mouthed and she shrugged.

After more hushed discussion between the judge and the defence barrister, the prosecutor was then called over and joined in the conversation. Finally, both barristers went back to their seats. The jury looked as confused as I felt and some of them had started chatting among themselves.

The judge banged his gavel and silence descended on the court once more.

'The Crown has been advised that there has been a change of plan,' he said. 'Mr Hughes has informed me that his client wishes to change her plea.'

'She would now like to plead guilty to all charges.'

Patsy and I looked at each other in confusion.

Had I heard that right? Brianna had suddenly decided to plead guilty?

I didn't quite believe it. We watched, barely daring to take a breath as the judge asked if the Crown would accept Brianna's guilty plea.

'The Crown will,' nodded the prosecution barrister.

The jury broke out into excited chatter. The judge banged his gavel again.

'In light of Briana's guilty plea, court is dismissed,' he said. 'I'd like to go on record to say it's disappointing that Briana didn't make this decision before preparations were put in place for a full trial.

'The court is adjourned until a later date for pre-sentence reports.'

Patsy and I looked at each other, aghast.

'I was not expecting that,' she gasped.

'Me neither,' I said.

I wondered how Lee was feeling and whether he'd been told the news. As we walked out of the court, he was waiting outside the entrance.

I could tell by his face that he knew.

'I can't believe it,' he sighed. 'It's over. It's really over. She's admitted that she hurt me.'

His relief was palpable. However, he was angry too.

'Why did she put us all through those months of worry and change her mind at the last minute?' he ranted. 'She wanted to torture and control me and Bobby right until the end.'

'Try to focus on the positives,' Patsy told him. 'It's highly likely that she's going to go to prison now.'

However, I still had a question preying on my mind.

'Has she just admitted Actual Bodily Harm against Lee or the child cruelty charges relating to Bobby too?' I asked.

I was worried that we would still have to go through that trial and he would have to give evidence.

'The CPS have confirmed that she has pled guilty to all charges,' said Patsy. 'All that happens now is that they'll prepare pre-sentence reports and then there will be a sentencing hearing, probably in a few weeks' time.'

I'd never felt so relieved. It was really over for both Lee and Bobby. All that was left now was for Brianna to be punished.

'Can I come and see Bobby?' asked Lee. 'I want to be the one to tell him that she's admitted it.'

'I don't see why not,' nodded Patsy. 'I think it should come from you. You've been through it together. What do you think, Maggie?'

'I think that sounds like a great idea,' I smiled.

We arranged for both Patsy and Lee to meet us at my house after I'd picked Bobby up from school.

I didn't mention anything to Bobby as I didn't want to alert him to the fact that anything was wrong.

'Look, there's Dad,' he shouted as we drove down our road and saw Lee waiting outside. 'And Patsy.'

'Oh yes,' I said. 'They must have come round for a cup of tea.'

We all went into the kitchen and I put the kettle on.

'I've got us all some doughnuts as a special treat,' I smiled, putting a box on the table.

'Bobby, Dad has come round today to tell you something really important,' Patsy told him.

'What is it?' asked Bobby anxiously.

'No, it's good news, son,' said Lee, trying to reassure him. He took a deep breath.

'Brianna went to court today and she admitted everything,' he said. 'She told the judge that she had hurt you and me and everyone believed us.'

Bobby didn't show any reaction.

'Is she going to get into trouble for hurting us?' he asked. 'Will she get told off?'

'She's going to get really told off,' nodded Patsy. 'She might even go to prison because the judge and the police are so cross about what she did to you and Dad.'

I could see Bobby's little mind trying to process it and take it all in.

'That's good that they believed us,' he nodded.

'It's really good, Bobby,' smiled Lee. 'Brianna can't hurt us any more. We're finally free.'

TWENTY

Safe and Loved

It had been a stressful day at court so I was determined to do something nice. When Patsy had left, I suggested that we all went out to McDonald's for tea.

'Yay!' grinned Bobby.

He and Lee chatted away as he tucked into his Happy Meal.

They talked about school and playing football and something Bobby had seen on TV.

Lee was taking a bite out of his Big Mac when Bobby suddenly turned to him.

'Dad, did Brianna hurt you too, like she hurt me?' he asked.

I could see Lee hadn't been expecting this and he looked surprised.

'Yes, Bobby,' he said. 'She did. Can you remember that you used to see me sometimes with a black eye or cuts and bruises?'

'Yes,' nodded Bobby. 'From when you were fighting in the pub.'

'No son, they wasn't from the pub,' Lee told him. 'That's what Brianna said to people to cover up the fact that she had done them to me.'

Bobby took a slurp of his milkshake.

'I was really frightened of her, Bobby,' Lee told him. 'Just like you were.'

I could tell Bobby was listening and taking it all in.

'Is that why you couldn't stop her from hurting me?' he asked.

Lee nodded. I could see the shame on his face.

He put down his burger and reached across the table for Bobby's hand.

'I'm so sorry, son,' he said, tears filling his eyes. 'As long as I live, I will always regret not protecting you from her. But things have changed now. She's admitted what she did to us both. You're safe and I swear I won't ever let that happen to you again.'

'Brianna's not going to hurt us no more is she, Dad?'

Lee shook his head.

'No, Bobby. The police have said that she's probably going to go to prison.'

'For a long, long time?' asked Bobby.

'Yes,' nodded Lee. 'For a long, long time.'

I felt tears prick my own eyes as I watched father and son hold hands across the table. Bobby was finally realising that Lee was vulnerable too and he was slowly learning to forgive his dad.

A couple of weeks later, I got a message from Patsy to say that Brianna's sentencing was taking place at the end of that week. When I saw Lee at the contact centre that evening, I talked to him about it.

'Are you going to go back to court?' I asked him. 'I'm happy to come with you again if you want some support?'

He shook his head.

'I ain't gonna go this time,' he said, much to my surprise.

I had thought that he'd want to attend in order to get closure.

'Brianna's ruled enough of my life,' said Lee. 'I don't want her taking up any more of my time. Now she's admitted it, I don't want to ever see her again or even think about her. Bobby and I need to move on with our lives.'

'That's fair enough,' I said.

The police had promised to update Patsy about the outcome.

'I honestly hope they lock her up and throw away the key for everything that she did to us,' said Lee, with feeling.

That Friday afternoon Patsy called to tell me that Brianna had been sentenced.

'DC Orton just rang me from outside court,' she said.

'How did it go?' I asked.

'She got six years,' she replied. 'Four years for Actual Bodily Harm and two for child cruelty.'

'I'm glad,' I sighed. 'I hope she never hurts anyone ever again.'

It didn't seem like a long sentence to me, but it was enough for Bobby and Lee to begin to move on with their lives.

What I still found hard to understand was where this hatred for Bobby and Lee had come from. Why had she felt the need to treat them that way? We knew that she was capable of loving and caring for a child, as both Melodie and Poppy had been well looked after. I felt for them too in all of this as I knew they missed Brianna. I wondered what would happen to them now.

'How did Lee take the news?' I asked Patsy.

'He was relieved but surprisingly calm,' she replied. 'I think he's more focused on the assessment now.'

Lee's eight-week parenting assessment was due to come to an end shortly and I knew it was on his mind. The last few weeks of contact had been a lot more flexible and fun for him and Bobby. They were hardly going to the contact centre now apart from the odd session with an assessment worker. Lee had taken Bobby bowling and now we were moving into spring and the evenings were getting lighter, this afternoon after school he had taken him to the park.

'Have you had fun?' I asked as Bobby came running through the front door.

'Why don't you come in for a cuppa?' I asked Lee.

I could see that he looked exhausted and on edge.

'What's going on, Lee?' I asked him as I put the kettle on. 'What's bothering you?'

'What's going to happen, Maggie?' he asked. 'When will I know whether I've passed this stupid assessment? I was never no good at exams – what if I fail? What if they take Bobby away from me?'

I could see he was getting anxious and, to be honest, it was understandable. Things seemed to be going well but we didn't know what was going on behind the scenes at Social Services and there was never a 100 per cent guarantee that he would be awarded full-time parental responsibility for Bobby.

'I'm worried that after all my problems and how I treated Bobby, they'll say it's in his best interests to stay living with you. Or they'll extend it again.

'Don't get me wrong, I do like you and all, Maggie,' Lee said, 'but I want Bobby back with me.'

'I understand,' I smiled. 'And if anyone asks me, I'll be saying that I agree with you 100 per cent.

'Let's see what happens at the meeting.'

We had a meeting looming at Social Services where they would make a final decision on the assessment. There weren't as many people there as there had been at the LAC Review: Lee and I, and Patsy and her manager, a woman in her fifties called Julie. She had quite a stern face and an abrupt manner and I could see Lee was nervous because he didn't know her. Julie was chairing the meeting.

'Welcome everybody,' she smiled. 'And thanks for coming, Lee.

'All of the reports are in and I've spent the past few days going through them,' she said, flicking through the bundle of papers that she had in her hand. 'Palvi's passed on her comments from the contact sessions and I've also had comprehensive reports from assessment workers who have had sessions with Lee and Bobby and spoken to Lee separately as well.'

Lee shifted uncomfortably in his seat.

'I've also spoken to Patsy and Maggie and got their thoughts about how best to move forwards.'

'And?' asked Lee impatiently. 'What did they say? I promise you, I'm trying really hard with my mental health and I ain't had any panic attacks for ages. I just want the best for my lad, I really do.'

'Lee,' said Patsy kindly, placing her hand on his. 'Listen to Julie.'

She continued.

'Lee, I'm so pleased to hear that the legal proceedings concerning Brianna are all over and she was given a custodial sentence.'

'Thank you,' he nodded.

'I've gone over all of the reports and looked closely at what everyone has said and there was only one conclusion I could reach.'

Julie paused and turned to Lee.

'Lee, it's clear that you pose no risk to Bobby. In fact, everyone has commented on how devoted you are to your son.'

'I swear I am,' said Lee. 'I know I let him down but I've promised that I'm going to make it up to him.'

'We all know that clearly you were being abused too, and were trapped in a violent relationship and it's admirable that you've been trying to work through those issues,' added Julie. 'I'm delighted to say that nobody has any issues about Bobby returning to live with you full-time. We feel that it's in Bobby's best interests to be with his dad.'

'Well done, Lee,' smiled Patsy.

I could see Lee was in shock. He stared at Julie in disbelief.

'What do you mean?' he asked. 'Did I pass it? Can I have Bobby back?'

'You passed,' smiled Julie. 'And with flying colours. Your son can come home.'

'Oh that's wonderful news!' I exclaimed. 'I'm so happy for you both.'

I couldn't stop myself from getting up and giving Lee a big hug.

'Lee, you're shaking,' I said.

'I think I'm in shock,' he gasped. 'I wanted this so, so much but I never really thought it would happen.'

'We don't expect you to have to cope alone though,' Julie told him. 'Patsy will still keep in touch with you and we can offer you support as and when you need it.'

'I'm just so happy. I can't wait to tell Bobby!'

Lee and Patsy were sitting on the sofa in my living room when Bobby and I walked in the door from school.

'What are you doing here?' he asked, looking puzzled.

'Come and sit down, Bobby,' Patsy told him. 'Your Dad's got some good news for you.'

Lee couldn't stop smiling.

'What is it, Dad?' he asked. 'What's happened?'

'You're coming back to live with me, son,' he said. 'Social Services says it's OK.'

At first Bobby didn't show any reaction.

'What is it?' Lee asked him. 'I thought you'd be pleased.'

'I don't want to live in that funny house with the broken windows and all the rubbish outside,' he said in a quiet voice.

Lee laughed.

'The hostel?' he replied. 'No, don't you worry, son, I would never take you there.'

'You and Dad are going to have your own place,' Patsy explained. 'The council is going to help Dad get a flat.'

'You'll even get your own bedroom,' Lee told him.

Bobby looked at me for reassurance.

'Isn't that wonderful news?' I smiled. 'Daddy just found out today and he wanted to be the one to tell you.'

Finally, Bobby smiled.

'Can we paint my new bedroom red cos I support Liverpool?' he asked and everyone laughed.

'Whatever you want, son,' Lee told him. 'Whatever you want.'

Now they knew he was going to have Bobby full-time, Social Services had supported Lee's application to the council for a two-bedroom property. Lee received a letter from them confirming that Bobby was returning to live with him. His GP had also backed up his application. Ten days later, there was good news.

'We've got a flat!' he told me. 'I get the keys in a couple of hours. Can I take Bobby to come and look round it? I want him to get excited too.'

'Course you can,' I replied.

He came round that night after school.

'I'm got a surprise for you,' he told Bobby.

'Is it a present?' he asked.

He'd learnt by now that sometimes presents were for him.

'It's kind of a present,' said Lee, jangling the keys in front of Bobby.

'It's the keys to our new flat. Would you like to come and see it with me?'

Bobby's face lit up.

'Can Maggie come too?' he asked. 'If she's gonna come and see me, then she needs to know the way.'

'Oh, you and Daddy should go together,' I smiled.

'No, Maggie, if Bobby wants you there then you should be there,' said Lee firmly.

I drove us there. It was about forty minutes from my house and fifteen minutes from Bobby's school.

'This is a lovely road,' I said as we drove down the street of Victorian terraces.

'Here it is,' said Lee.

It was the ground floor of one of the terraces. Lee put the key in the lock and turned it. We went through the entrance hall and opened the door to the flat. It was cold and dark inside.

'I don't like this,' whispered Bobby, reaching for my hand.

Lee fumbled for the lights. The doorway led straight into a front room. The walls were painted a sickly peach colour and there was an old blue carpet on the floor, but the ceilings were high and there was a large bay window.

'This is a lovely big room,' I said. 'And it will look a lot more cosy with some furniture in it and some nice ornaments and pictures.'

'Patsy said Social Services would give me some stuff like a fridge and beds and a washing machine,' said Lee.

As he'd left Brianna's house with nothing except a couple of carrier bags, he was having to start again.

'I wanna see my bedroom,' said Bobby.

What I assumed would be Lee's room was next to the living room, then there was a box room at the back.

'Is this mine?' asked Bobby and Lee nodded.

It was a small room with wood-chipped walls that were painted in a grubby magnolia colour, but Bobby looked delighted.

'How about you and I give it a lick of paint one weekend?' suggested Lee. 'And you'll have to choose a duvet cover for your new bed.'

'I get a bed?' asked Bobby, obviously delighted.

'Of course you do,' nodded Lee. 'When you're with me you'll always have a bed to sleep on, son.'

I could see these snippets of their old life were hard for Lee to hear. They just reminded him of what he and Bobby had been through and I could tell that he still felt guilty about that.

After we'd looked around some more, we left Lee there as he wanted to stay and make a list of what they needed while Bobby and I headed home.

'What do you think of your new flat?' I asked him.

'It's nice,' he said. 'I like my bedroom.'

'Are you happy to be moving in with Daddy again?' I said. He nodded.

'Dad's like he was before,' he smiled. 'I remember now.'

'Before Brianna?' I asked and Bobby nodded.

'He's going to be like that dad again,' he nodded. 'I liked that one.'

And hearing that, I knew that Bobby had learnt to trust his dad again.

A couple of days later, my agency had a coffee morning for foster carers. I'd only been there a few minutes when I felt a tap on my shoulder.

'Hi Maggie,' said a familiar voice.

It was Sue.

'I was actually going to ring you this week,' she told me.

She explained that Melodie and Poppy were leaving her house in just over a week.

'They're going to live with their birth dad and their stepmum,' she said. 'It's a long way away and they're nervous, but I think it's the best thing for them, given the circumstances.'

She explained that she'd taken them to see Brianna in prison and they'd had a tearful goodbye.

'They'll still visit her, but it won't be more than every few months,' she said. 'How's little Bobby doing?'

'He's doing really well,' I said. 'He's moving back in with Lee and they've just got a council flat.'

'Aw, I'm glad it worked out for them,' she replied. 'They deserve it after everything they've been through.'

Sue explained that she was going to have a little goodbye party for the girls at her house.

'I know Poppy would love it if Bobby could come,' she said.

I knew Bobby would miss Poppy and it was important that he had a chance to say goodbye, but I was still a little apprehensive. 'What about Melodie?' I asked. 'I know Bobby will be less keen to see her.'

'If you're there then I'm sure Melodie will keep her distance and I'll read her the riot act and make sure she stays away from him as well,' Sue assured me.

'I'll see what Bobby says,' I told her.

That was the first question Bobby asked when I told him about the party.

'Melodie will be there but Sue and I will be keeping a close eye on her so don't you worry,' I said, but I could see that he was still anxious.

On the day of the party, he was very quiet and clingy and wouldn't leave my side. Sue had done a buffet and there were a few of her family members there and some of the girls' friends from school.

We'd only been there for about half an hour but I could see Bobby had had enough.

'Shall we go now?' I whispered and he nodded eagerly.

'Let's go and say bye to Poppy,' I told him.

We went over. They were quite shy around each other.

'Bobby's going to really miss you, Poppy,' I told her.

Bobby stared at the ground.

'I hope you and Melodie are really happy at your dad's house,' I added. 'You take care.'

I gave her a hug but I didn't want to force Bobby to do that.

'Bye Pops,' he said shyly.

'Patsy said maybe you can send me a letter sometimes,' she told him.

He nodded.

'Oh, maybe I can borrow Maggie's phone and ring you?'

She nodded.

'I got you a goodbye present,' he said shyly.

I got it out of my handbag and passed it to him – it was a photo of him, Melodie and Poppy that had been taken at my house and I'd put into a frame.

Melodie had kept her distance from Bobby but I felt it was important that I acknowledged her and said goodbye to her.

'Good luck, flower,' I told her. 'I hope you're really happy with your dad.'

'We'll be fine,' she said. 'He's got a very big house.'

'Well at Dad's flat I've even got my own bed,' said Bobby proudly.

I waited for the nasty comment back from Melodie but it didn't come.

'That's nice, Bobby,' she said.

★

A few days later, it was time for our own goodbye. Lee had been working hard to get the flat all ready for them. It still looked a little sparse but I'd helped him cobble together some furniture we'd found in local charity shops and on Facebook. Every few days, Bobby and I would drop some more of his things over there.

We'd arranged with Patsy that his last day with me would be Saturday, then I would drop him over to Lee on Sunday morning.

'What do you want to do on your last day?' I'd asked him.

Bobby had mulled it over.

'Can we see Edie?' he'd asked.

We spent the morning packing his things. He'd only been with me for three months so he didn't have a huge amount of stuff.

I peeled off all the certificates stuck to the fridge. There was a bravery certificate for his swimming, a reading award from school and a certificate to say well done for being a library monitor. It was wonderful to see all the progress Bobby had made.

'Don't forget these,' I told him.

'Do you think Dad will let me put them up at our new house?' he asked.

'I'm sure he will,' I replied. 'I know how proud he is of you.'

When everything was packed, that afternoon we drove over to Louisa's house. Edie was standing at the upstairs window.

'Look!' shouted Bobby. 'Edie's waiting for me!'

'Yes, she is,' I smiled. 'She really loves you.'

Louisa had made us a lovely tea of quiche, chips and salad and Bobby spent the next couple of hours playing babies with Edie.

'I bet you're going to miss him,' Louisa said as we had a cup of tea together.

'I am,' I nodded. 'But you know me, I've done this enough times to know that I can't let myself dwell on it.'

I couldn't help but get attached to children, and Bobby, and everything that he had been through, had really touched my heart.

As a foster carer, I knew the only way to get through this was to focus on the positives. Bobby was going home to his dad. It was the best possible outcome for both of them and I was delighted. I had to put my own feelings to one side.

'Before you go, Edie's got a little present for you,' said Louisa.

She handed Edie a box and she ran over and gave it to Bobby.

'What is it?' he asked.

'You'll have to open it and see,' I told him.

He ripped the paper off to find a LEGO tank set.

'Maggie told me how much you like LEGO,' Louisa told him.

'Thank you, Edie,' he grinned, patting her on the head.

Soon it was time for Edie to have her bath and get ready for bed.

Bobby gave her a cuddle.

'Bye Edie,' he said sadly. 'Maybe I'll see you again one day.'

'Well, when you and Dad come and visit me, perhaps Edie can pop in too?' I suggested and he nodded enthusiastically.

That night I tucked him into bed for the last time.

'Just think, this time tomorrow you'll be in your new bed at your new house with Daddy,' I smiled.

He nodded.

'I like this bed too,' he said quietly.

'I know you do, lovey,' I said, ruffling his hair.

I couldn't help but think how far he had come from that silent, scared child who had turned up on my doorstep on that cold winter's night. I knew that he was leaving a very different boy.

'I'm going to miss you a lot,' I told him. 'And I'm so proud of you.'

'Are you?' he asked.

'I certainly am,' I replied. 'I'm proud of you and of Daddy and I know you're going to be so happy together.'

He nodded.

'Will we see you again?' he asked.

'If you want to, then of course you will,' I told him. 'Daddy's got my phone number so you can both ring me any time you like and maybe in a few weeks when you're settled you can come round for tea.'

Bobby gave me a smile.

Soon it was time for lights out as we had a busy day tomorrow.

I went back downstairs, made myself a cup of tea and sat at my laptop to do my final recordings, my heart heavy with sadness.

On the morning a child left my house, it was always busy. I liked it that way as it meant there was little time for tears or sadness.

'Right, your case is already in my car,' I told Bobby. 'Do you want to have a look round the house just to check that we've not forgotten anything?'

We were in the car on the way to Lee's by nine-thirty.

As we pulled up outside the flat, I could see Lee was waiting at the window.

'Look, there's Dad,' I told Bobby. 'He can't wait to see you.'

He came out to help us take in the boxes while Bobby ran in to see his bedroom.

'Oh wow,' I heard him gasp.

'Dad's put some Liverpool pictures on the wall and I've got a Liverpool duvet.'

'That's great,' I smiled.

'I wanted to make it nice for him,' Lee said.

After we'd brought Bobby's stuff in, Lee gave me a quick tour. He'd done a brilliant job and everything looked so much brighter with a lick of paint.

'Would you like a cuppa?' he asked.

'No thanks, I'm going to get going and leave you and Bobby to it,' I told him.

I took a deep breath and prepared myself to say goodbye.

'Bye Bobby,' I told him, giving him a big hug. 'This isn't really a goodbye though because we're going to see each other very soon.'

'Bye Maggie,' he said quietly.

'You look after Daddy,' I told him.

Lee walked me outside.

'I don't know what to say,' he sighed. 'Thank you doesn't seem enough for all you've done for us.'

'Thank you is absolutely fine,' I smiled. 'Look after yourselves and enjoy being a dad to your gorgeous boy.'

Just then, I heard a tapping on the glass and I looked around to see Bobby waving from the front window. I swallowed the lump in my throat and waved back.

He stood and watched as I got in my car and drove off down the road.

It was only when I was out of sight that a tear rolled down my cheek.

Despite the sadness I felt when a child left my home, all I could do was focus on the positives. Now they were free of Brianna, I knew Lee and Bobby were going to have a happy life together and I could tell Lee truly loved his son. The pain and the sadness of everything they'd been through wasn't going to disappear overnight, but I was confident they could work through it and heal together.

Bobby was leaving my house knowing that he was loved, that he was cared for and that he was safe. And I knew that was all I could ask for.

Acknowledgements

Thank you to my children, Tess, Pete and Sam, who are such a big part of my fostering today – I had not met you when Louisa came into my home.

To my wide circle of fostering friends – you know who you are! Your support and your laughter are valued. To my friend Andrew B for your continued encouragement and care.

Thanks also to Heather Bishop, who spent many hours listening and enabled this story to be told, my literary agent Rowan Lawton and to Anna Valentine, Vicky Eribo and Beth Eynon at Seven Dials for giving me the opportunity to share these stories.